D0558881

On Heaven
and Earth

JORGE MARIO BERGOGLIO–
ABRAHAM SKORKA

On Heaven and Earth

POPE FRANCIS *on* FAITH,

FAMILY, *and the* CHURCH *in the*

TWENTY-FIRST CENTURY

TRANSLATED BY
Alejandro Bermudez and Howard Goodman

EDITED IN SPANISH BY
Diego F. Rosemberg

EDICIÓN DEFINITIVA, SEIX BARRAL,
BUENOS AIRES, 1995.

B L O O M S B U R Y
LONDON • NEW DELHI • NEW YORK • SYDNEY

A Burns & Oates book

Bloomsbury Publishing Plc
50 Bedford Square
London WC1B 3DP

www.bloomsbury.com

Bloomsbury Publishing, London, New Delhi, New York and Sydney

First published 2013

Translation © 2013 by Image, a division of Random House, Inc.

Originally published in Spanish as *Sobre el cielo y la tierra* by
Editorial Sudamericana S.A.®, a division of Random House
Mondadori, Argentina in 2010. © 2010, Editorial Sudamericana S.A.

© 2010 Cardenal Jorge Mario Bergoglio
© 2010 Rabino Abraham Skorka
© 2010 Random House Mondadori, S.A.

All rights reserved.

A CIP record for this book is available from the British Library.

ISBN 978 1 4729 0381 5

Printed and bound in Great Britain by
CPI Group (UK) Ltd, Croydon, CRO 4YY

10 9 8 7 6 5 4 3 2 1

First Edition

CONTENTS

HOW WE EXPERIENCE DIALOGUE
Abraham Skorka

"And G-d said to them . . ."[1] It's the first recorded conversation we encounter in the Bible. Humans are the only creatures to whom the Creator speaks in this manner. In the same section of Genesis we are shown that each of us has a special capacity to relate to nature, to our fellow man, to ourselves and to G-d.

Of course, these relationships which man is inclined to form are not like watertight compartments which are independent of one another. Our relationship with nature results from our observations and the detailed handiwork that we observe; relationships with our fellow man are based on our interests and life experiences; and our relationship with G-d, which comes from deep inside our being, is a result of self-

1 Genesis 1:28

dialogue, and is nurtured by all the other relationships mentioned above.

True dialogue is at the heart of the thinking man's life and demands that each person tries to get to know and understand the person with whom they are conversing. As Ernesto Sabato expressed in his unique style in the prologue to his book *One and the Universe*,[2] "One sets off for distant lands, or seeks the knowledge of man, or investigates nature, or searches for G-d; only afterwards does he realize that the phantom he was chasing was Himself."

When conversing with one's fellow man, words are merely vehicles for communicating, although, even in societies where everyone speaks the same language, the exact same words can take on somewhat different meanings. Each person adds their own nuance to many of the words they use, which then become part of the linguistic heritage. Dialogue requires that each participant become acquainted with the other person.

"G-d's candle is man's soul which reveals the innermost parts of his being."[3] In its most profound sense, to have a conversation is to bring one's soul nearer to another's in order to reveal and illuminate his or her core.

2 *Uno y El Universo* Edición definitiva, Seix Barral, Buenos Aires, 1995
3 Proverbs 20:27

When a dialogue reaches this level of magnitude, one becomes aware of what he or she has in common with the other person. He or she each has the same persistent existential questions with their various interpretations. Each soul is a reflection of the other. The Divine Breath, which both possess, knows to unite the two and then form a link with Him that will never weaken, as it is written, "A cord of three strands is not quickly torn apart."[4]

There were many different opportunities which helped pave the long road of details and circumstances that brought Cardinal Bergoglio, and me closer and allowed us to get to know each other better.

One day we set a time and place so that we could just sit together and talk. The topic of discussion was life itself as seen through the prisms of local society, global concerns and the evidence of villainy and nobility that surround us. We spoke with complete intimacy, if you don't count the presence of G-d. Although His name wasn't brought up consistently (perhaps it should have been?), we felt that He was always present.

The meetings became recurring events, with each one focused on a different topic. One time, our meeting took place at my office in the synagogue and I was commenting on some of the framed documents that

4 Eccleciastes 4:12

adorn the walls. I paused to focus on some pages from a manuscript written by the great thinker Rabbi Abraham Joshua Heschel and some of the other texts as well. Regardless, my friend had stopped following me, having spotted a greeting that I had hung next to the Heschel documents. He had presented it at the synagogue some years before on the occasion of the Jewish New Year. While I went about re-arranging some things in my constantly cluttered workspace, I saw that he continued to focus on those particular pages, which he himself had signed and dated.

Curiosity seized me. What was going through his mind at that moment? What was so special about what I had done, above and beyond caring for and displaying a document that I consider a valuable testimony of what interfaith dialogue can accomplish in our world? I did not ask him. Sometimes, there are moments of silence that, in themselves, constitute a sort of answer.

Shortly thereafter, we chose the Archbishop's office for one of our meetings. The conversation turned toward the presence of religious sentiment in Latin American poetry. He told me, "I have a two volume anthology on this that I would like to lend you, please stay here while I go to the library to find them." I then found myself alone in his small study. I looked over at the bookshelf and its accompanying photos and I imagined that these must be people he truly cares for—those who mean a lot to him. Suddenly, I noticed among them a framed picture that I had given to him as a gift. The photo was of the two of us and had been taken at one of our meetings.

I was struck speechless. I had found the answer to my earlier question.

It was at that meeting that we decided to write this book.

Although every rabbi makes a special commitment to G-d during his training, once he begins his work as a teacher of the Law he has the obligation to set an example, more than any other Jew, to show people how one must fulfill their obligations to the Creator. Just as the prophets had done after experiencing moments of spiritual elevation while alone, the rabbi should go back to the people and teach them based on this acquired spirituality. After all, the dimensions of spiritual life that one attains by oneself only acquire meaning, according to biblical teachings, when they are used to help uplift others.

Regardless of the fact that rabbis communicate more frequently using the spoken word, there's always an underlying challenge to capture and refine those ideas so that they can be put on paper. A spoken word can become blurred or distorted over time. Written ideas become permanent testimonies that allow more people to access them.

When I'm with Cardinal Bergoglio, these two lessons become one. During our chats, the main topic and focus of concern was, and continues to be, individual people and their problems. We let the conversations flow spontaneously as opposed to following written agendas. As such, giving expression to our intimate conversations in book form meant that we each had to take turns strengthening the bonds between us. We have transformed our dialogue into a group conversation, exposing our souls. We accept all of the risks this implies, yet remain profoundly convinced that this is the only way for us to understand what it means to be a human being, moving ever closer to G-d.

THE FAÇADE AS A MIRROR
Jorge Bergoglio

Rabbi Abraham Skorka, in one of his earlier writings, made reference to the façade of the Metropolitan Cathedral that depicts the encounter between Joseph and his brothers. Decades of misunderstandings converge in that embrace. There is weeping among them and also an endearing question: Is my father still alive? During the times of national organization,[5] this was the image they proposed, and not without reason. It

5 Ed. Note: The national organization (organización nacional) marks a period in Argentina's history between 1852 and 1880. During this time, a national constitution was approved that defined the federal nature of the government. Education and communications were also dramatically expanded. Although regarded as a time that forged Argentina's strength and identity, it also came with social upheaval.

represented the longing for a reuniting of Argentineans. This scene aims to work to establish a "culture of
encounter." Many times I alluded to the difficulty that
we as Argentineans have to consolidate that "culture of
encounter;" instead it seems that we are seduced into
dispersion and the abysses that history has created. At
times, we are better able to identify ourselves as builders of walls than as builders of bridges. We lack the
embrace, the weeping and the question about the father, for our patrimony, for the roots of our Fatherland.
There is an absence of dialogue.

Is it true that we Argentineans do not want dialogue? I would not say it that way. Rather I think that
we succumb to attitudes that do not permit us to dialogue: domination, not knowing how to listen, annoyance in our speech, preconceived judgments and so
many others.

Dialogue is born from a respectful attitude toward
the other person, from a conviction that the other person has something good to say. It supposes that we can
make room in our heart for their point of view, their
opinion and their proposals. Dialogue entails a warm
reception and not a preemptive condemnation. To dialogue, one must know how to lower the defenses, to
open the doors of one's home and to offer warmth.

There are many barriers in everyday life that im-
pede dialogue: misinformation, gossip, prejudices,
defamation, and slander. All of these realities make up

a certain cultural sensationalism that drowns out any possibility of openness to others. Thus, dialogue and encounter falter.

But the façade of the Cathedral is still there, like an invitation.

Rabbi Skorka and I have been able to dialogue, and it has done us good. I do not remember how our dialogue started, but I can remember that there were no barriers or reservations. His simplicity was without pretense, and this facilitated things. I could even ask him jokingly, after a loss by River Plate, if that day he was going to eat "hen soup."[6]

When he proposed to me that we publish some of our dialogues, my "yes" was spontaneous. Reflecting later, in solitude, I thought that the explanation for this quick response was due to our experience of dialogue during quite a bit of time; a rich experience that consolidated a friendship and that would give testimony of our walk together from our distinct religious identities.

With Rabbi Skorka I never had to compromise my Catholic identity, just like he never had to with his Jewish identity, and this was not only out of the respect that we have for each other, but also because of how

6 Ed. Note: River Plate is one of the most popular soccer teams in Argentina. Its Archrival is Boca Juniors. Eating "hen soup" (*cazuela de pollo*) is equivalent to the English expression "eating crow."

we understand interreligious dialogue. The challenge consisted in walking the path of respect and affection, walking in the presence of God and striving to be faultless.

This book is a testimony to that path. I consider Rabbi Skorka a brother and a friend; and I believe that both of us, through these reflections, never stopped looking with the eyes of our heart at the façade of the Cathedral, so eloquent and promising.

On Heaven
and Earth

1. ON GOD

SKORKA: It has been many years since we first met and a brotherly bond has been forged between us. While studying the books of the Talmud, I found one that says that friendship means sharing meals and spending time together, but in the end it points out that the sign of a real friendship is the ability to reveal what is in one's heart to the other person. That is what happened over time with the two of us. I believe that undoubtedly the most important thing that brought us together was, and still is, G-d, who caused our paths to cross and allowed us to open our hearts to each other. Although we broached many topics during our regular conversations, we never spoke explicitly about G-d. Of course, it was always understood that He was present. It would be good to start this exchange, which we plan to leave as a testimony of our dialogue, by discussing Him who is so important in our lives.

BERGOGLIO: What a great word: *path*! In my personal experience with God I cannot do without the path. I would say that one encounters God walking, moving, seeking Him and allowing oneself to be sought by Him. They are two paths that meet. On one hand, there is our path that seeks Him, driven by that instinct that flows from the heart; and after, when we have encountered each other, we realize that He was the one who had been searching for us from the start. The initial religious experience is that of walking: walk to the land that I am going to give you.[7] It is a promise that God makes to Abraham. In that promise, in this, in this walking, an alliance is established that consolidates over time. Because of this I say that my experience with God takes place along the path, both in the search and in allowing myself to be sought, even if it may be by diverse paths–of pain, of joy, of light, or of darkness.

SKORKA: What you have said reminds me of a few biblical verses. For example, when G-d tells Abraham: "Walk in my presence and be blameless."[8] Or when the prophet Micah needed to explain to the Israelites what G-d wanted from them, and he tells them to "do justice

7 Genesis 12:1
8 Genesis 17:1

and to love goodness, and to walk humbly with your G-d."[9]

Without a doubt, experiencing G-d is dynamic, to use a word that we learn in our mutual study of basic science.[10] However, what do you think we can say to people nowadays when we find the idea of G-d to be so mangled, profaned and diminished in importance?

BERGOGLIO: What every person must be told is to look inside himself. Distraction is an interior fracture. It will never lead the person to encounter himself for it impedes him from looking into the mirror of his heart. Collecting oneself is the beginning. That is where the dialogue begins. At times, one believes He has the only answer, but that's not the case. I would tell the people of today to seek the experience of entering into the intimacy of their hearts, to know the experience, the face of God. That is why I love what Job says after his difficult experience and the dialogues that did not help him in any way: "By hearsay I had heard of you, but now my eye has seen you."[11] What I tell people is not to know God only by hearing. The Living God is He that you may see with your eyes within your heart.

SKORKA: The Book of Job teaches us a great les-

---

9 Micah 6:8
10 Abraham Skorka is a doctor of chemistry, and Jorge Bergoglio is a chemical technician.
11 Job 42:5

son because—in short—it says that we can never know how G-d reveals Himself in specific circumstances. Job, a just, upright man, wanted to know why he had lost everything, even his health. His friends told him that G-d had punished him for his sins. He responds by saying that even if he had sinned, he had not been *that* bad. Job is comforted only when G-d appears to him. His questions are not answered, but the touch of G-d's presence stays with him. We can find several things in this story that shape my personal perception of G-d. First, Job's friends show themselves to be arrogant and nonsensical by espousing the theory that "You have sinned, therefore G-d has punished you," transforming G-d into some sort of computer that calculates reward or punishment. At the end of the story, G-d tells Job—who had railed so much against the injustices of his Creator—that he should intercede and pray for his friends, because they had spoken falsely about Him.[12] Those who had cried out in suffering, demanding heavenly justice, were pleasing in G-d's eyes. Those who insisted on a simplistic view of G-d's nature were detested by Him. As I understand it, G-d reveals Himself to us subtly. Our current suffering might be an answer for others in the future. Or, perhaps we ourselves are the response to something from the past. In Judaism, G-d is honored by

12 See Job 42:7–8

our compliance with the precepts that he revealed. As you mentioned, each person and each generation must find the path on which they can search for and feel His presence.

BERGOGLIO: Exactly. We receive creation in our hands as a gift. God gives it to us, but at the same time He gives us a task: that we subdue the Earth. This is the first form of non-culture: what man receives, the raw material that ought to be subdued to make culture– like the log that is transformed into a table. But there is a moment in which man goes too far in this task; he gets overly zealous and loses respect for nature. Then ecological problems arise, like global warming, which are new forms of non-culture. The work of man before God and before himself must maintain a constant balance between the gift and the task. When man keeps the gift alone and does not do the work, he does not complete his mission and remains primitive; when man becomes overly zealous with his work, he forgets about the gift, creating a constructivist ethic: he thinks that everything is the fruit of his labor and that there is no gift. It is what I call the Babel syndrome.

SKORKA: In rabbinic literature, there is a question as to why G-d did not like the Tower of Babel. Why did he halt construction by making people speak different languages? In reading the text, the simplest explanation is that the attempt to build a tower reaching Heaven was part of a pagan religion. The act was an expression of arrogance toward G-d. The *Midrash*[13] states that what really bothered G-d was that the builders were more concerned about losing a single brick than with losing a man who might fall from such a great height. The same thing happens now–there is a tension between the gift and the work. There needs to be a perfect equilibrium because man needs to progress so that he can become more human. Even though G-d is the one who planted and created everything, man is the focus of the material world and the greatest divine work. The way we are living today, the only thing that matters is the success of our economic system, and what is least important is the well-being of mankind.

BERGOGLIO: What you have said is brilliant. The Babel syndrome is not only a constructivist posture, but there is also the appearance of a confusion of languages. That is typical of situations in which there is an exaggeration of the mission, ignoring the gift, because in that case pure constructivism carries with it the lack of dialogue that at the same time entails aggression, misinformation, and annoyance . . . When one reads Maimonides[14] and Saint Thomas of Aquinas,

13 The Midrash is a group of homiletic texts from wise men of the Talmud, presenting non-literal interpretations of the Bible. 14 Ed. Note: Maimonides, born Moses ben Maimon (1138–1204), is regarded as the greatest Jewish philosopher and rabbi of the medieval period. He combined religious Jewish tradition with Aristotelian philosophy, especially in his masterpiece, *The Guide for the Perplexed.*

two nearly contemporary philosophers, we see that they always start by putting themselves in the position of their adversary in order to understand them; they dialogue from the standpoint of the other.

SKORKA: According to the Talmudic interpretation, Nimrod was a Babylonian dictator who held a tight grip on everything, and that is why the people spoke only one language–his. This tyrant ordered the construction of a tower that would reach Heaven in order to leave his mark, and thus, presumed rather arrogantly to be physically closer to G-d. The point of building was not to benefit mankind. The betterment of people's lives held no importance. By building only for themselves while using one despotic language and not a universal one, each person was punished by being made to speak a language that no one else could understand. This is a very important story and it is always incredibly relevant.

2. ON THE DEVIL

BERGOGLIO: The Devil is, theologically, a being that opted not to accept the plan of God. The masterpiece of the Lord is man; some angels did not accept it and they rebelled. The Devil is one of them. In the book of Job he is the tempter, the one that looks to destroy the work of God, he that brings us to self-sufficiency, to pride. Jesus defines him as the Father of Lies, and the book of Wisdom says that sin entered the world through the Devil's envy of God's masterpiece. His fruits are always destruction: division, hate, and slander. And in my personal experience, I feel him every time that I am tempted to do something that is not what God wants for me. I believe that the Devil exists. Maybe his greatest achievement in these times has been to make us believe that he does not exist, and that all can be fixed on a purely human level. Man's life on

8

Earth is warfare; Job says it meaning that people are constantly put to the test; that is to say, a test to overcome a situation and overcome oneself. Saint Paul took it and applied it to athletes that compete in an arena and who must deny themselves many things in order to achieve success. The Christian life is also a sort of sport, a struggle, a race where one has to detach oneself from the things that separate us from God. Beyond this, I want to point out that the Devil is one thing. It is quite another matter to demonize things or people. Man is tempted, but there is no need to demonize him.

SKORKA: There is a wide variety of opinions on this topic in Judaism. In Jewish mysticism there is what is called "the other power"–something that can be likened to evil forces. Although the well-known primal image of the snake that appears in the Bible can be interpreted as an evil force that incited man against G-d, in the case of Job's Satan, as well as the one that appears to Baalam, it is more of a hypostasis of G-d. In Job's case, Satan presents G-d with the doubts that surface in our own minds when we see an upstanding man thanking G-d when he lacks for nothing. If He blesses a man with everything, why would that person not be thankful to G-d? Would he do likewise in a time of distress? In Baalam's case, when he was hired by Balak to curse the Israelites,[15] Satan placed himself in front of Balaam so that he would not disobey G-d's

15 Numbers 22

command to deny the King of Moab's request. When we talk about the manifestation of good and evil in creation, to me, the verse that explains it best appears in the book of Isaiah[16] where it says that G-d forms the light and creates darkness and that He makes peace and creates evil. It is a very complex verse, which I interpret to say that darkness does not exist in and of itself, but as the absence of light. Likewise, evil occurs when good is removed from a situation. It also cannot exist by itself. I prefer to talk about instincts rather than angels. For me, it is not about an external force so much as it is something within man that challenges the Lord.

BERGOGLIO: In Catholic theology there is also an internal element that we can explain with the fall of nature after original sin. We agree on what you call instinct, in the sense that when someone does something inappropriate it is not always because the Devil encouraged it. Someone can do something bad through his own nature, by "instinct," which is encouraged by an external temptation. In the Gospels it is striking how Jesus starts his ministry with forty days of fasting and prayer in the desert, and it is in that moment that Satan tempts him with stones that he can turn into bread, with the assurance that nothing would happen to him if he threw himself from the temple and with promise that he would have anything he wanted if

16 45:7

Jesus would just adore him. That is to say, the Devil uses the existential situation of fasting and proposes to Jesus an "omnipotent way out," centered in himself (a satisfying, vain and prideful way out) that would take Jesus away from his mission and identity as Yahweh's Servant.

SKORKA: In the end, accepting the general concept of evil is up to the free will of each individual. All the rest depends on our perceptions and interpretations of the texts that we consider sacred. What remains clear is that something exists, whether it is instinct or the Devil, which presents itself as a challenge for us to overcome so that we can uproot evil. We cannot be ruled by evil.

BERGOGLIO: That is precisely man's battle on Earth.

3. ON ATHEISTS

BERGOGLIO: When I speak with atheists, I will sometimes discuss social concerns, but I do not propose the problem of God as a starting point, except in the case that they propose it to me. If this occurs, I tell them why I believe. But that which is human is so rich to share and to work at that very easily we can mutually complement our richness. As I am a believer, I know that these riches are a gift from God. I also know that the other person, the atheist, does not know that. I do not approach the relationship in order to proselytize, or convert the atheist; I respect him and I show myself as I am. Where there is knowledge, there begins to appear esteem, affection, and friendship. I do not have any type of reluctance, nor would I say that his life is condemned, because I am convinced that I do not have the right to make a judgment about the honesty of that person; even less, if he shows me those human virtues that exalt others and do me good. At any rate, I know more agnostic people than atheists; the first are more uncertain, the second are more convinced. We have to be coherent with the message that we receive from the Bible: every man is the image of God, whether he is a believer or not. For that reason alone everyone has a series of virtues, qualities, and a greatness of his own. If he has some vileness, as I do, we can share that in order to mutually help one another and overcome it.

SKORKA: I agree with what you have said; the first step is respecting your fellow man. But I would add one more point of view. When a person says, "I am an atheist," I believe he or she is taking an arrogant position. He who doubts has a more nuanced position. An agnostic thinks that he or she has not yet found the answer, but an atheist is 100 percent convinced that G-d does not exist. It is the same arrogance that leads some to assert that G-d definitely exists, just like the chair I am sitting on. Religious people are believers, but we do not know for certain that He exists. We can perceive Him in an extremely profound sense, but we never see Him. We receive subtle replies from Him. According to the Torah, Moses was the only person to have spoken directly, face to face, with G-d. As for everyone else–Jacob, Isaac, etc.–the presence of G-d appeared to them in dreams or by some messenger. Even though I personally believe that G-d exists, it is arrogant to say that He exists as if it were just another certainty in

13

life. I would not casually affirm His existence because I need to live the same humility that I demand of the atheist. The right thing to do would be to point out–as Maimonides did in his thirteen principals of faith–that "I believe with complete faith that G-d is the Creator." Following Maimonides' line of thought, we can say what G-d is not, but we can never be sure of what G-d is. We can talk about His qualities and attributes, but in no way can we describe His form. I would remind the atheist that the perfection of the natural world is sending us a message. We can gain an understanding of how it works, but not its essence.

BERGOGLIO: The spiritual experience of encounter with God is not controllable. One feels that God is there, one has the certainty, but he cannot control God. We are made to subdue nature; that is what God commands. We cannot, however, subdue our Creator. As a result, in the experience of God there is always an unanswered question, an opportunity to be submerged in faith. Rabbi, you said one thing, which in part, is certain: we can say what God is not, we can speak of His attributes, but we cannot say what He is. That apophatic[17] dimension, which reveals how I speak about

17 Ed. Note: *Apophatic* is a term that refers to an intellectual approach to God through what is known as "negative theology." Through this way, one attempts to describe God by what He is not, that is, what may not be said about His perfect goodness ("God is unknowable"). It stands in contrast with cataphatic or "positive" theology.

God, is critical to our theology. The English mystics speak a lot about this theme. There is a book by one of them, from the thirteenth century, *The Cloud of Unknowing*, that attempts again and again to describe God and always finishes pointing to what He is not. The mission of theology is to reflect and explain religious facts, and among them, God. I would also classify as arrogant those theologies that not only attempted to define with certainty and exactness God's attributes, but also had the pretense of saying who He was. The book of Job is a continuous discussion about the definition of God. There are four wise men that elaborate this theological search and everything ends with Job's expression: "By hearsay I had heard of you, but now my eye has seen you."[18] Job's final image of God is different from his vision of God in the beginning. The intention of this story is that the notion that the four theologians have is not true, because God always is being sought and found. We are presented with this paradox: we seek Him to find Him and because we find Him, we seek Him. It is a very Augustinian game.

SKORKA: I believe with complete faith that G-d exists. As opposed to the atheist who is sure that He does not exist and does not entertain any doubts, I implicitly reveal a margin of uncertainty by using the word "faith." At a minimum, I have to acknowledge what Sigmund Freud wrote: that we need the idea of

18 Job 42:5

G-d to temper our existential angst. Nevertheless, after having done an in-depth analysis of positions that negate the existence of G-d, I still believe. When my work was done, I still felt G-d's presence. I retain a certain amount of doubt in any case since this is an existential problem and not a mathematical theory, although there is some room for doubt in mathematical theories as well. That said, when we think about G-d we have to do so with special terminology. Everyday logic does not apply. Maimonides put forth that idea long ago. Agnostics will continue to create their famous paradoxes. For example, if G-d is omnipotent, surely He could create a rock that He Himself could not lift; but if He created such a rock, that would mean He is not omnipotent. G-d is above and beyond any logic and its paradoxes. Maimonides explains that He knows everything in its complete form. We have only limited knowledge. If we had the same understanding that G-d has, we would be gods ourselves.

4. ON RELIGIONS

SKORKA: Each person's relationship with G-d is unique. Is it not true that each of us has different personalities, different preferences and different life experiences? Each person's relationship and dialogue with G-d is special. The various religious traditions also exert their own influence on that dialogue. People often ask, "Why are there different religions?" I believe the answer is that individuals have different experiences. A religion is formed when a common denominator is found as these different experiences are shared. In Judaism's case, since it is a religion that is thousands of years old, it needs to be interpreted in ancient terms. In Rome, there was a differentiation between religion, the nation and the people. In Judaism, the origin of which predates that of Rome by about a thousand years, the three concepts are indivisible. To be a part of the Jewish people means having to accept its religion, as Ruth declared to Naomi, "Your people shall be my people and your G-d, my G-d."[19] In addition, Judaism contains the concept of being "the chosen people," which causes a lot of confusion. Abraham had an encounter with G-d that resulted in them creating a pact, and Abraham committed his offspring to its fulfillment. The core of the agreement was that the people would maintain an ethical standard based on precepts that G-d was going to reveal to them so that they could then testify to G-d's presence in man's reality. As Amos said, "You alone I have known, among all the families of the Earth; therefore I will punish you for all your iniquities."[20] In Chapter 9, Verse 7, the same prophet states in G-d's name, "Are you not like the Ethiopians to me, O Israelites?–oracle of the LORD–Did I not bring the Israelites from the land of Egypt as I brought the Philistines from Caphtor and the Arameans from Kir?" We are the people specifically chosen by G-d for the task, and each generation must choose to renew this pact with Him. Unfortunately, those that hate us label us as a people that believe ourselves to be a "superior race," to paraphrase the Nazi definition of their own people, while at the same time they considered Jews to be an "inferior race." Christianity expanded the

19 Ruth 1:16
20 Amos 3:2

concept of "the people of Israel" to include all those that embrace its own faith as well.

BERGOGLIO: God makes Himself felt in the heart of each person. He also respects the culture of all people. Each nation picks up that vision of God and translates it in accordance with the culture, and elaborates, purifies and gives it a system. Some cultures are primitive in their explanations, but God is open to all people. He calls everyone. He moves everyone to seek Him and to discover Him through creation. In our case, that of Judaism and Christianity, we have a personal revelation. God Himself encounters us; He reveals Himself to us, He shows us the way and He accompanies us; He tells us His name, He guides us through the prophets. Christians believe, ultimately, that He manifested Himself to us and gave Himself to us through Jesus Christ. Moreover, throughout history, there have existed circumstances that created schisms and constructed diverse communities that have different ways of living Christianity, like the Reformation. We lived through a thirty year war and it shaped different faiths. It is very hard to accept and it was a disgraceful time, but that is the reality. God is patient, He waits, and God does not kill. It is man that wants to do so on God's behalf. To kill in the name of God is blasphemy.

SKORKA: How can it be that there are people who speak poorly of others that practice a different religion if those others are sincere and are trying to help people get closer to G-d? Those that present themselves as knowing the absolute truth, judging everyone else and their actions with condescension, have gotten used to the frequent practice of this disgraceful pagan principle. Paganism is a central theme in biblical literature. When ancient Israel performed sacrifices on Yom Kippur,[21] they needed to take two goats. Tradition says that the goats needed to be as similar as possible.[22] One would be sacrificed to G-d, while the other would be sacrificed out in the desert, carrying with it the sins of the people. This naturally begs the question, "Does G-d really need sacrifices?" Maimonides[23] thought that men felt they ought to do it as a show of gratitude, and G-d conceded them the opportunity to get closer to Him in that way—but with certain limitations. For example, there were no human sacrifices. Since men felt the need to express themselves with offerings, He regulated them. Getting back to the previous topic, when I study this aspect of the Yom Kippur ritual, I wonder, "Why did the two goats need to be similar?" The answer I found was that sometimes one might find different things packed in the same wrapping. One can speak in the name of G-d and use clothing that symbolizes purity or spiritually uplifting actions, yet from under this same mantle the worst things can ooze out.

21 Leviticus 16
22 Mishnah Yoma 6:1
23 *The Guide for the Perplexed,* part III, chap. 32

Sometimes there is a fine line between the pagan and the pure. During the twentieth century, deadly passions were ignited in the masses by the use of methods that some considered religious rituals. At that time, G-d was pushed aside.

BERGOGLIO: To kill in the name of God is to make ideological the religious experience. When this happens, political maneuvering enters and a divinization of power emerges in the name of God. Those who do it are people that construct themselves as God. In the twentieth century they devastated entire nations because they considered themselves God. The Turkish did it with the Armenians, the Stalinist Communists did it with the Ukranians, and the Nazis with the Jews. They used a discourse of divine attributes to kill people. It really is a sophisticated way of killing people through the use of an inflated ego. The second commandment proposes that you love your neighbor as yourself. No believer can limit the faith to himself, his clan, his family, or his city. A believer is essentially someone who goes into an encounter with other believers, or non-believers, to give them a hand. The Bible in this sense is impressive; the Prophet Amos is a scourge to those who commit injustices to their brothers, to those who do not go out and help, to those who do not bring the presence of God to the poor and to the destitute. There also appears in the law the concept of "gleaning." What is that? The book of Ruth describes it when it says that you should not return to a field already harvested because what remains must be left for the widow and the orphan.

SKORKA: The Bible teaches us the idea that we are all descendants of the first man. In other words, we are all linked to each other in brotherhood. One should never be indifferent to another human being. The whole Bible perhaps is simply a demand–do not be indifferent to spirituality, to G-d or to your neighbor. What then is the social function of religion?

BERGOGLIO: Let us go back to the first two commandments: the first is you shall love your God with all your heart and with all your soul; the second one is you shall love your neighbor as yourself. Jesus says that in these two commandments the entire law is contained. Hence, the liberal conception of religion being allowed only in places of worship, and the elimination of religion outside of it, is not convincing. There are actions that are consistently done in places of worship, like the adoration, praise and worship of God. But there are others that are done outside, like the entire social dimension of religion. It starts in a community encounter with God, who is near and walks with His people, and is developed over the course of one's life with ethical, religious, and fraternal guidelines, among others. There is something that regulates the conduct of others: justice. I believe that the one who worships God has, through that experience, a mandate of justice toward his brothers. It is an extremely creative justice because it invents things: education, social progress, care and attention, relief, etc. Therefore, the integral religious man is called to be a just man, to bring justice to others. In this aspect, the justice of religion, or religious justice, creates culture. The culture made by a woman or a man that worships the living God is not the same culture made by the idolater. John Paul II had a very bold phrase: a faith that does not produce culture is not a true faith. He emphasized this: creating culture. Today, for example, we have idolatrous cultures in our society: consumerism, relativism, and hedonism are examples of this.

SKORKA: Worship only makes sense when it is practiced with others; if not, it is not worship. What and whom exactly are we worshipping? This is an essential question. That is why I always say that priests and rabbis have to get their hands dirty. Religious services are only part of what makes up a religion. A sanctuary that is not filled with life and does not help people to sustain their lives is a part of the pagan culture.

BERGOGLIO: I do not have any doubt that we must get our hands dirty. Today, priests no longer wear their cassocks. But a recently ordained priest used to do it and some other priests criticized him. So he asked a wise priest: "Is it wrong that I wear my cassock?" The wise priest answered him: "The problem is not if you wear a cassock or not, but rather if you roll up its sleeves when you have to work for the good of others."

SKORKA: Religions are dynamic and in order not to become outdated they must be in permanent contact

with the outside world. What does not change about a
religion is its set of values. In the end, every society is
created based on the answer to three questions: How
does that society perceive G-d, man and nature? Judaism claims that G-d is an eternal being, that the most
important creature created by G-d is man, and that
nature is something He created from nothing. This is
the unique idea that differentiates Jewish from Greco-
Roman thought, which contained a theogony, a religious mythology, where many gods fought amongst
themselves and, after arriving at Olympus, they involved themselves slowly with the lives of men. The
novelty that Judaism brought to the world is the belief
in only one purely spiritual G-d. As a result, the revelation came–when G-d showed Himself to man and the
people of Israel in particular–and then came the Torah, a combination of legal principles laid out in plain
language that was readily understandable. It is not a
text that is meant to be definitive. When someone studies the Talmud, one discovers that what they are debating is how this or that rabbi interpreted the different
precepts of the Torah. That is why, in Judaism, there
is always a constant evolution and rethinking of ideas.
Now I want to stress that what cannot be changed are
the handful of principles that represent its values.
Someone who only cares that a religious service con-
sists of certain words or that a ceremony is performed
in a certain manner has maintained a very important
tradition, but it is just a façade if it is not accompanied

by a life of justice, honesty and love. That person is just opting for the wrapping—a beautiful package that contains nothing of substance. A Hasidic rabbi used to say, "I do exactly what my father did and I essentially have the same values. But my father was my father, and I am me. His life experiences are useful to me in part, but only in part."

BERGOGLIO: I agree that what is essential is conserved through the witness and testimony of the fathers; in our case, through the apostles. In the third and fourth centuries the revealed truths of faith were theologically formulated and transmitted as our nonnegotiable inheritance. That does not mean that throughout history, through study and investigation, other insights were not discovered about these truths: such as what Christ is like, or how to configure the Church, or how and what should be true Christian conduct, or what are the commandments. All of these are enriched by these new explanations. There are things that are debatable, but—I repeat—this inheritance is not negotiable. The content of a religious faith is capable of being deepened through human thought, but when that deepening is at odds with the inheritance, it is a heresy. At any rate, religions refine certain expressions with time, even though it is a slow process because of the sacred bond that we have with the received inheritance. This respect is such that we must be very careful not to mess it up by going too quickly. One medieval theologian expressed in this way the progress and comprehension of inheritance, the received revelation: "The legitimate rule of all progress and the correct standard of all development consist in the inheritance being consolidated through the ages, developed with passing of the years and expanded with the passage of time." To respond with the received inheritance to the new issues of today takes time and even more when issues of conscience are concerned. When I was a boy, a divorcee could not enter your home, and even less so if they were remarried. Today, the Pope himself summons those that are in a new union to live in the Church. He asks them to pray, to work in the parish communities, and to participate in works of charity. Just because they are on the margin of the commandment does not erase their baptism. I admit that the tempo cannot keep up with the speed of social change, but holy leaders, those that seek the voice of God, have to take the necessary time to find the answers. Nevertheless there is the risk of confusing other economic, cultural and geopolitical interests. It is important to know how to distinguish.

5. ON RELIGIOUS LEADERS

SKORKA: With regards to someone who wants to become a religious leader, I am sure we will agree that the key word is vocation. If the vocation is not there, there is nothing. The other word that we often emphasize is tradition. The vocation to serve G-d emerges from a profound process of introspection; from discovering one's self, deepening relationships with one's fellow man, and perceiving messages in nature. When we are teenagers searching for a path to guide us in life, we discover the spiritual dimension of G-d during these various experiences and, as a result of that discovery, some decide to make a supreme pledge to G-d. As soon as one functions as a spiritual guide, the challenge is to serve G-d by committing oneself to his or her fellow man. According to the story of Genesis,

God made man in His likeness and image. To be the likeness or image of something means that there is some reference point to the original. On seeing one's neighbor, one should see G-d. It is not just a theoretical aid, but practical as well. That being said, many years of teaching have taught me that we need to be very careful with those who have chosen to dedicate themselves to a spiritual path. This is because unfortunately history teaches us that there are many people that have rejected the fundamentals of spirituality and still held themselves out as spiritual guides, only to lead their flock into abominable disasters like those at Waco and Guyana. We have to be extremely cautious with those who believe themselves to be the supposed redeemers of others.

BERGOGLIO: I agree with the word vocation; in our tradition it is crucial. When God makes Himself known, He does it with a calling: "Go forth from your land, your relatives, and from your father's house to a land that I will show you."[24] God gets in the way. God calls, and that's what we see in the vocation of the great leaders. In our tradition, a mission always starts with a calling. There is a case that always strikes me, that of the Gerasene demoniac. Jesus expels the demon from him and later the man wants to follow him. Jesus tells him no, that instead, he is to remain in his land and tell the local people what happened to him. Jesus, in a

24 Genesis 12:1

28

certain way, proposes to him: "Proclaim the wonders of God to your people." It is because of this that the word *vocation* is essential. There can also be rejections or refusals to the calling or to the vocation. In the Gospel, the most common classic example is the rich young man. Jesus looks upon him with sympathy, he loves him and tells the young man that if he would like to follow him more closely, he must sell all that he has, give it all to the poor and follow him. The young man becomes very sad, and does not do it because he is rich. Jesus invites him, he calls him, but the young man is not moved to take that step; it is a thwarted calling. In the Gospel, Jesus says: "It is not you who have chosen me, but I who have chosen you." It is necessary to have a key initial discernment; it is what we call in Christian Spirituality the right intention. In other words, with what intention you arrive; it is not that someone would come with a bad intention as an imposter, but there are unconscious motivations that can turn into fanaticism or other things. During the formation process, one must purify the right intention, because nobody, not even those who discover themselves called, responds with complete integrity; the response is a mixture because we are all sinners.

SKORKA: There is a very interesting paragraph in the Book of Deuteronomy[25] that guides us on how to distinguish between a false prophet and a real one.

25 13:2–6

The Talmud says that even a false prophet can produce supernatural signs as a proof of what he claims. That paragraph from Deuteronomy is very important. It says that a false prophet is one that wants to lead you to stray from the paths of G-d, of justice, and of respecting life, and it describes a multitude of tests to determine whether that is the case. What then can the congregant do when faced with a leader that sometimes, whether knowingly or not, leads his community to ruin by using enormous psychological power wrapped in religious language? There are different sections of the Bible that deal with this and whose message is to be careful; stay away from that which would conquer your heart and close you in its grasp in order to control your mind and desires. Coming back to the paragraph in Deuteronomy that I alluded to earlier—each individual should examine the core of any prophet's message. If it is not in harmony with justice, grace and peace, his message is a false one and should be rejected. One of the ways in which a congregant can tell if someone wants to restrict their interior freedom and enslave them is if the leader speaks with absolute certainty–"G-d told me this and this is the way it has to be." The same goes for teachers that act as if everything they say is absolutely correct. If they do that, you cannot trust them. Lessons of faith are transmitted with humility. There always has to be room for doubt. In Chapter 27 of the Book of Jeremiah, where G-d tells the prophet that the people must continue to withstand the yoke of Nebuchadnez-zar, He orders Jeremiah to put a yoke on his own shoulders as a sign to the people that they should not plan any kind of revolt. Shortly thereafter, another prophet, Hanania ben Azur, appears. He removes the yoke from Jeremiah and breaks it. Jeremiah did not stop him by telling him that G-d had said to do something different, he accepts Hanania's act. Jeremiah then turned around, went back to his private life, and spoke again with G-d who reconfirmed that what he had originally said was correct; that the people should continue to bear the yoke of the Babylonian empire. This shows us two things. The first is that G-d is dynamic and can change His mind. The Bible says, "Go back to G-d so that G-d may change His decree." This is the message of the book of Jonah. We cannot talk about G-d and His messages in absolute terms; acts of faith include suggesting differing interpretations raised by doubt. The other concept that this story teaches us has to do with the most important term that should define a religious leader–the only virtue that the Torah explicitly applies to Moses–humility. Any religious leader that is prideful and lacks humility, who talks arrogantly and in absolutes, is not a good religious leader. A leader who is arrogant, who does not know how to deal with people, who repeatedly says, "I am," should not be a religious leader.

BERGOGLIO: But there are, there are. "Say it to me,

Ma'am," it was said in my time by Catita, the character done by Niní Marshall.[26] I like what you said about doubt, because that goes directly to the experience that anyone has if one wants to be just in the presence of God. The great leaders of the people of God were men that left room for doubt. Going back to Moses, he is the most humble character that there was on Earth. Before God, no one else remained more humble, and he that wants to be a leader of the people of God has to give God His space; therefore to shrink, to recede into oneself with doubt, with the interior experiences of darkness, of not knowing what to do, all of that ultimately is very purifying. The bad leader is the one who is self-assured, and stubborn. One of the characteristics of a bad leader is to be excessively normative because of his self-assurance.

SKORKA: Doubt is a necessary requirement of faith. In fact, faith arises from our feelings of doubt. I sense G-d, I feel Him, I have spoken with Him many times, but what is essential to our faith is that we keep looking for Him. I can be 99.99 percent certain about Him, but never 100 percent; we spend our whole life seeking

26 Ed. Note: Niní Marshall is the artistic name of Marina Esther Traveso (1903–96), considered by many to be the most famous female Argentinean playwright and comedian. One of her most famous characters was Catalina or "Catita," an Italian immigrant who constantly gossiped about friends and neighbors.

Him. For Jews, faith is created by that very same doubt. After the Holocaust, we asked ourselves how G-d could have abandoned us. If He represents complete justice, why did He not intervene? Does He not always accompany the righteous and those who suffer? Those are the same questions that Job had when he asked G-d why his sons had died, why he lost his health and why he had lost everything despite being a good and just man. In each case, G-d's response was, "I have my reasons which are unknowable to man, with whom doubt will always remain."

BERGOGLIO: I have always been enticed by Job's phrase that I have already mentioned: "By hearsay I had heard of you, but now my eye has seen you."[27] After being tested, one sees things differently, growing in understanding. Taking up the theme of religious ministers, humility is what gives assurance that the Lord is there. When someone is self-sufficient, when he has all the answers to every question, it is proof that God is not with him. Self-sufficiency is evident in every false prophet, in the misguided religious leaders that use religion for their own ego. It is the stance of religious hypocrites because they speak about God, who is above all things, but they do not put into practice His commands. Jesus said to the faithful, referring to such people: "Therefore, do and observe all

27 Job 42:5

33

things whatsoever they tell you, but do not follow their example."[28]

SKORKA: We need to constantly teach by example. We have to instill a sense of humility in those who choose to become religious leaders and try to constantly drum into them that what they have chosen to do is a holy act.

In my congregation, we have a youth group and I tell the kids who are going to be the leaders of the various sections that they have a very special mission. First, they need to know the theories regarding how children should play together so that they can have the best time possible. They also have to teach the children social values so that they learn how to get along with each other. However, if these were the only lessons that we taught, there would not be any difference between our leaders and those of any non-religious group. That is why I tell them that above all they are obligated to expose the children to the religious way of life. Their mission is one of holiness, therefore it should contain a spiritual component that is established through prayer and rituals tailored so that they make sense to children. These group leaders definitely help the rabbi with his or her work. Aside from that, all those who are in a position of leadership have to realize that they should not impose their personal problems onto their

28 Matthew 23:3

job and they should never believe too much in themselves because of their position of leadership. When I talk to people who need help because they are ill or distressed, I always tell them, "Let us see what *my* boss says." I never hold myself out as someone who has special powers because I am a rabbi. One time, I had just finished officiating a wedding and a couple who I had married eight years ago came over to greet me. The first thing I thought to ask was whether they had children and they told me that, unfortunately, the wife had miscarried her pregnancies. I took their hands and said to them, "Be strong and have faith." After some time had passed, the woman finally had a little girl and they returned to the synagogue for the traditional baby naming ceremony. Once the ceremony was over, they came up to me and asked if I remembered that I had given them advice on how to go on by being strong and having faith. I made it clear that I had sent them good vibes, as they say today, but that they should not believe that my words were what caused their successful pregnancy. All I did was petition G-d. Some of those who were there joked that I should publicize what happened so that the synagogue would be flooded with congregants and donations.

BERGOGLIO: The Rabbi healer!

SKORKA: No way. Sure, I believe that individuals can exhibit a spiritual force that helps the sick, but the miracle comes from G-d, never from man. Hasidic

35

tradition[29] teaches us that the Talmud[30] says that the world is sustained by the presence of thirty-six righteous men. However, as soon as any of them believe themselves to be righteous, they no longer are.

BERGOGLIO: A natural distrust comes over me when these phenomenal healers appear, even when revelations appear and visions; these things put me on the defensive. God is not a sort of Andreani[31] that sends messages all the time. It is different when a believer says that he is feeling something. Nevertheless, one has to admit that throughout history prophesies have existed and continue to exist. A place has to be left for someone whom God has chosen as a prophet, with the characteristics of a prophet. These, however, are not the people that normally say they bring a note from heaven. I have had to denounce many cases in Buenos Aries, because they are more common and frequent than one would believe. To think that what you or I feel as spiritual consolation when we pray is a prophecy or a revelation for the entire world would be very naïve. At times, there are things that people feel,

29 Hasidicism is a Jewish movement born in Eastern Europe in the eighteenth century. It has a very rich mystical content and it helps revitalize the faith of its members through canticles, dances, and traditions.
30 Babylonian Talmud, Sanhedrin, 97, b
31 Ed. Note: Andreani is the largest Argentinean express mail carrier.

and because of a poor interpretation or because of an unstable psyche, some confuse it with a prophecy. A short time ago I had a woman on the telephone who said she had a message for all Argentineans, and that I had to authorize her to tell everyone "for the salvation of us all." She sent me the message and I saw that there were things that were not right, there were inaccuracies and mistakes. I told her I could not authorize it. She insisted and disagreed with me and even without my authorization was going to transmit the message privately. There are people who feel a sort of prophetic vocation. Another issue, easier to interpret, is healing. Through scientific studies, some oncologists believe that there is psychological influence over the physical, some of these things can be explained. There also exists the ministerial intercession of a rabbi or a priest who prays or asks for the health of another and it is granted. What gives credibility to a person who is healing according to the law of God is simplicity, humility and the absence of a spectacle. Otherwise, instead of healing it can become a business.

SKORKA: I agree 100 percent. If someone uses their powers for entertainment, they are not truly religious and they are inventing a lie. There are a lot of people who follow trends that look to the beyond for answers to their physical and social problems. One has to be aware that when they go to see a rabbi–and I am sure that the same happens with priests–they are going to get an answer based on faith. It is not the same as a doctor's answer. We should never hold ourselves out as doctors. If someone comes to me about a health issue, I can help them by saying kind, soothing words, but at the same time I tell them that they need to keep following their prescribed medical treatment to the letter.

BERGOGLIO: For that, God gives us the instruments.

SKORKA: That reminds me of an old story. There was a flood, and a man was stuck on the roof of his house yelling for help. Almost immediately, a canoe came by to rescue him, but he refused to get in. "I am going to stay here because G-d's going to help me," he said to the oarsman. Later on a firefighter's lifeboat came by to save him and again he refused to get in. "No way—I'm staying here because G-d will save me," he repeated. Then, a police helicopter came to the rescue but he refused to climb aboard saying the same thing, "G-d will save me." In the end, the man dies and when he gets to heaven, he complains to G-d, "Why didn't you help me? You let me die!" At that point, G-d gets furious with the man. "What do you mean I did not help you? I sent a canoe, a lifeboat and a helicopter and you did not take any of them!"

BERGOGLIO: Very good, Rabbi. I would like to take up again the issue of leadership. I maintain that the leadership from a congregation cannot be equated to the leadership of an NGO (Non–Governmental Organization). I like very much a word that you used a little while ago: holiness. That is the command from God to Abraham. The word *holiness* is like a springboard to the transcendent. In an NGO, the word *holiness* does not fit. Yes, there has to be a socially acceptable conduct, honesty, an idea of how the NGO is going to carry out its mission, and an internal policy. It can run phenomenally inside of a secular setting, but with regards to religion, holiness is unavoidable for a leader.

SKORKA: There is no doubt that anyone who leads a congregation has to be an honest person who works in pursuit of justice and acts accordingly. One of the more challenging aspects of a religious leader's job is mediation—interceding in people's affairs in order to achieve peace. In the Bible, it is done by interceding with G-d on behalf of the people. It is what Abraham did when he bargained with G-d to save the righteous of Sodom and Gomorrah, cities He condemned due to the iniquity of those that lived there. He bargained with God to save human lives. This attitude is completely different from the unhealthy, craven desire to exercise absolute and arbitrary power that we see so often! We saw the most terrible example of this in the great dictatorships of the twentieth century. Some studies of human behavior and social interaction are of the opinion that the totalitarian movements of the twentieth century such as Nazism and Communism adopted certain features from religious institutions such as the use of symbols and mysticism.

39

It is common for the masses to dream of *saviors* that will resolve all of their problems and relieve their anxieties. These dreams have been used and manipulated by clever, evil individuals who seduce the people, conquering their hearts and minds so that in the end, the people can be led at the leader's whim. Argentina has suffered from this phenomenon for a long time. Our society tends to elect "saviors." That is why I think we can only have managers here and not leaders, because leaders conduct the country toward certain goals. Managers only administrate. True leaders are driven by values that sustain their work with an air of transcendence. They yearn to make history in the present, resolving future problems and serving as a model for future generations. Managers are only worried about the present. Another thing, if politics has anything to do with religion, it has nothing to do with G-d, of course, but both share the need to become involved with social problems. Politics and religion are two systems that deal with the same problem—man and his difficulties. Education is the people's only defense against leaders that would do them harm.

6. ON THE DISCIPLES

BERGOGLIO: A question that we should raise at this point is how we form and facilitate the growth of those that have decided to take up the religious path. Some believe that one, to be a priest, embraces the ecclesiastical career. Thankfully, that expression is no longer popular, because the word *career* gives the impression that there is a ladder, as if it were a business. Instead, everything is born from the fact that someone is called, summoned, touched by God. We base our formation on four pillars. The first is the spiritual life, where the aspirant enters into a dialogue with God, through the interior world. For that, the first year of formation is dedicated to understanding and putting into practice the life of prayer, the spiritual life. Afterwards, all of that continues, but with less intensity. The second pillar refers to community life; we do not even conceive of a solitary formation. It is essential to be "kneaded" and to grow in a community. Then a person will know how to guide it and how to direct it. To accomplish this, we have seminaries. In any community, these competitions and jealousies will appear, and that helps to open the heart and learn to make room for others. Such things are revealed even in the seminarians' soccer matches. Another pillar is the intellectual life; the seminarians are enrolled in the Theology Department, where there are six years of studies. Two are for philosophy, as a foundation for theology, and later there is dogmatic theology, developed by scholars: where God, the Trinity, Jesus, and the sacraments are explained. Furthermore, there are the biblical and moral theology courses. The fourth pillar is what we call apostolic life: the seminarians are assigned to a parish and go every weekend to help the pastor with ministerial issues. During the last year of formation, they live in a parish. We look at this final year of total dedication as an opportunity for both virtues and defects to emerge. In that moment things begin to emerge more clearly that need to be corrected as well as those things that need to be promoted in their personality, their charisma. We say that those four pillars need to interact and influence one another.

SKORKA: In Judaism, it is not easy to train someone to be a rabbi because the source texts that the students have to learn are in Hebrew or Aramaic, and the classes are in Hebrew. Moreover, as soon as the seminarians possess a considerable knowledge of the basics, they go to work as rabbis' assistants due to a shortage of religious leaders. Of course, as part of our curriculum we also have subjects such as Philosophy, Bible, Talmud, History, and Biblical Criticism. Since the Seminario Rabínico de Latinoamérica belongs to the Conservative[32] movement, we deal with a very broad spectrum of knowledge and interpretation of the sources. We also study Hebrew literature from every era as well as other topics that have to do with pastoral work, such as Psychology, Sociology and Anthropology. Something that is very important to us is that everyone who comes to study at the seminary has graduated college or is working toward their degree.

BERGOGLIO: It is not necessary to have a university degree to be a Catholic seminarian. The degree will be acquired in Theology or Philosophy, but, in fact, it is increasingly common that there are university seminarians with a degree or with two or three years of work experience. We see that today, unlike before, older people are entering the seminary. The situation is much better because at the University of Buenos Aires you will get to know real life, the different points of view that exist, the different scientific approaches, a

32 The Jewish Conservative current teaches that customs and laws given by the tradition must be kept; nevertheless, unlike the very Traditionalist current, it keeps a deep and very dynamic intellectual dialogue with scientific development.

cosmopolitan perspective . . . it is a way to have your feet on the ground.

SKORKA: That is exactly why we demand it–so that the clerics have a sense of reality. It is ideal if their degree is in the humanities, but it is not a requirement. I myself have a doctorate in chemistry from the University of Buenos Aires. One can also know G-d through the perfection of His work. I saw myself becoming a researcher in any one of a variety of scientific fields, although I always liked Judaic studies. At some point, I threw myself into the teaching of Judaism. I had already officiated as a rabbi while studying for my doctorate. As Albert Einstein used to say, I would love to have G-d's blueprint for creating the universe. I do not believe there is a contradiction between science and religion. For me, the order that we have discovered in the world is a series of clues that G-d has given to man.

BERGOGLIO: We accept in our seminary, approximately, only 40 percent of those that apply, so the vocation has to be discerned. For example, there is a psychological phenomenon: pathologies or neuroses that seek external securities. There are some that feel that by themselves they are not going to be successful in life and look for organizations that can protect them. One of those organizations is the clergy. In this respect, we keep our eyes open, we try to know those who demonstrate interest, we give them in-depth psychological tests before they enter the seminary. Later, in the year of community life before they enter, during

44

weekend meetings, we can see and discern who has a vocation, and those who in reality are only seeking a refuge or were mistaken in their discernment of a vocation. Assuming all who enter have a vocation, there can also later be infidelity to that call. In the case of Saul: he was called and he betrayed the Lord.[33] An example would be the case of worldliness. Throughout history, there have been both worldly priests and bishops. One might think that having a woman on the side is being worldly, but that is only one of the double lives that are usually mentioned. There are those that seek to compromise their faith for political alliances or for a worldly spirituality. One Catholic theologian, Henri de Lubac, says that the worst that can happen to those that are anointed and called to service is that they live with the criteria of the world instead of the criteria that the Lord commands from the tablets of the law and the Gospel. If this were to happen throughout the Church, the situation would be much worse than those embarrassing periods with libertine pastors. The worst that can happen in the priestly life is to be worldly, to be a "light" bishop or a "light" priest.

SKORKA: The Jewish view also dictates that we should avoid being materialistic. A verse in the Talmud points out that the sages criticize those who seek to live life in the moment, for the here and now; those who

33 Saul did not obey God's precepts and commandments. See 1 Samuel 13:7–14; 15.

belittle and ignore the afterlife and transcendence–the belief that everything we do now affects the future. Up to here we agree, but I would ask–and here we find one of the differences between the Jewish and Catholic views–how should we handle this? At some point, the Catholic Church decided to make the maximum demand–total devotion by renouncing marriage and family. It asks one to live in this world without getting involved with worldly things. Here Judaism differs. It says, "You have to accept the challenge of living in the world and struggling with all the difficulties that modern trends bring to your doorstep while continuing to hold on to your values." Nevertheless, within the Jewish community there are very observant people who enclose themselves in their ghettos and deal with the outside world only for their basic necessities. I on the other hand, belong to the Conservative movement– although traditionalist is a better name–that suggests that Jews keep one foot in this world and deal with its problems, while holding fast to the idea that it is wrong to be materialistic. It is difficult to do, and right now it is one of the biggest problems in Judaism. Today, we do not live in ghettos anymore; we have changed and have become more cosmopolitan. The fight right now has become one of not getting caught up in what is trendy and sticking to the search for spirituality. The Catholic priest has an enormous challenge–mingling with the people without enclosing himself in an ivory tower. It is the same with traditional Judaism. The common challenge is to avoid being influenced by materialism though we have different ways of resolving the same root problem.

BERGOGLIO: I would like to make a clarification: a Catholic priest does not get married in the Western Tradition, but he can in the Eastern Tradition. There priests can marry before being ordained, but if they have already been ordained, then they cannot get married. The lay Catholic who lives in fullness of the faith goes down the same path that you stated. He is inserted in the world up to his neck, but without being carried away by the spirit of the world, and it is very difficult. Now, what happens with us who are consecrated? We are so weak that there is always the temptation to be contradictory. One wants to have his cake and eat it too, he wants the good things from the consecrated life *and* from the lay life. Before entering the seminary, I was on that path. But later, when one cultivates the choice for the religious life, he finds strength in that direction. At least I live it that way, which does not take away the possibility that at one point one could meet a woman. When I was a seminarian, I was enchanted by a young woman at my uncle's wedding. I was surprised by her beauty, the clarity of her intellect . . . and, well, I kicked the idea around for a while. When I returned to the seminary after the wedding, I could not pray during the entire week because when I prepared to pray, the woman appeared in my mind. I had to go back to thinking about what I was doing. I was still free because I was only a seminarian, I could have gone back home and said *see you later*. I had to think about my choice again. I chose once again–or allowed myself to be chosen for–the religious path. It would be abnormal for these types of things not to happen. When they do happen, one has to rediscover his place. He has to see if he reaffirms his choice or if he says, "No, what I am feeling is really beautiful, I am afraid that later I will not be faithful to my commitment, I must leave the seminary." When a seminarian thinks like that, I help him to go in peace, so that he can be a good Christian and not a bad priest. In the Western rite, to which I belong, priests cannot marry like the Catholic Byzantine, Ukrainian, or Greek rites. In these Churches, the priests can get married; the bishops cannot, they have to remain celibate. They are very good priests. Sometimes I tease them, I tell them that they have a woman in their house, but that they do not realize that they also got themselves a mother-in-law. In Western Catholicism, the issue has been discussed by some organizations. For now, the Church remains firm on the discipline of celibacy. There are those who say, with a certain pragmatism, that we are missing out on more manpower. If, hypothetically, Western Catholicism would change on the issue of celibacy, I believe that it would be for cultural reasons (like in the Eastern Church), not as much as a universal option. For the time being, I am in favor of maintaining celibacy, with the pros and the cons that it has, because it has been ten centuries of good experiences more often than failure. What happens is that the scandals are immediately seen. But tradition has weight and validity. Catholic priests chose celibacy little by little. Until 1100, there were those who opted for it and those who did not. Later, in the Eastern Churches, they continued the non-celibacy tradition as a personal option, and in the West it was the other way. It is an issue of discipline, not of faith. It can be changed. Personally, it never crossed my mind to get married, but there are cases. Think about the Paraguayan President Fernando Lugo, a brilliant guy, but as a bishop he fell and renounced his diocese. In this choice he was honest. Sometimes there are priests that fall into this.

SKORKA: And what is your position?

BERGOGLIO: If one of my priests comes to me and tells me that he has gotten a woman pregnant, I listen to him and help him to find peace, and little by little I help him realize that natural law comes before his right as a priest. Therefore, he must leave his priestly ministry and take care of his child, even though he might decide not to marry that woman. Because just as the child has a right to have a mother, the child also has the right to have the face of a father. I commit myself to do all the paperwork in Rome, but he must leave everything. Now, if a priest tells me that he got passionate,[34] that he had a fall, I would help him to

34 Ed. Note: He means passionate in a sexual sense.

get it corrected. There are priests that can be corrected and others that cannot. And, unfortunately, some do not even pose the issue to their bishop.

SKORKA: What do you mean by "corrected"?

BERGOGLIO: That they would do penance, that they would maintain their celibacy. The double life does not do us any good, I do not like it; it means sustaining deceit. Sometimes I tell them: "If you cannot deal with it, then make up your mind."

SKORKA: I would like to make a distinction between a priest who falls in love with a woman and confesses, and pedophilia, which is something completely different. It is a very serious problem that needs to be rooted out completely. It is another story if it is just two adults having an affair or falling in love with each other.

BERGOGLIO: Yes, but they need to correct the situation concerning pedophilia. We can rule out that celibacy carries pedophilia as a consequence. More than 70 percent of the cases of pedophilia occur in the family and in the neighborhood: grandparents, uncles, stepparents, neighbors. The problem is not linked to celibacy. If a priest is a pedophile, he is a pedophile before he is a priest. Now, when this happens, you can never turn a blind eye. You cannot be in a position of power and destroy the life of another person. In my diocese it never happened to me, but a bishop called me once by phone to ask me what to do in a situation like this and I told him to take away the priest's faculties, not to permit him to exercise his priestly ministry again, and to initiate a canonical trial in the tribunal that corresponds to that diocese. For me, that is the attitude to have; I do not believe in the positions that some hold about sustaining a certain corporate spirit so as to avoid damaging the image of the institution. That solution, I believe, was proposed at some point in the United States: to move priests from one parish to another. That is stupid because, in that way, the priest carries his baggage with him. The corporate reaction carries such a consequence, and because of that I do not believe in these ways out. Recently, in Ireland, they uncovered cases that occurred for twenty years, and the current pope clearly said: "Zero tolerance with this crime." I admire the courage and the straightforwardness of Benedict XVI on this point.

SKORKA: In Judaism we do not have the type of religious hierarchy that the Church does. Therefore, each congregation is on their own to monitor their religious leaders. There is an aphorism in Talmudic literature[35] that says, "Respect everyone, and suspect them as well." Every man has to struggle with his feelings and can make mistakes; therefore, congregations have to have some kind of control mechanisms in place where the rabbis keep watch over their disciples, and vice versa. When a rabbi is found to have behaved incorrectly, he should be removed from his

35 Derech Eretz Rabba 5

position if the gravity of the offense calls for it. At the Seminario Rabínico, we have seen the same thing that you pointed out earlier regarding the priesthood; there are people whose desire to join the rabbinate stems from psychological issues. That is why we also build confidential psychological profiles as part of the application process. We have to be very careful not to err about those to whom we give power and allow to be spiritual leaders of our congregations. During the 1970s, there was an accusation made against none other than Marshall Meyer,[36] the founder of the Seminario Rabínico and the Conservative movement in Argentina. I knew him when he was still suffering through all that. No one could deny that he had led a spiritual revolution in the Argentinean Jewish community as well as in Argentinean society in general. He put himself at risk by promoting human rights in the midst of a dictatorship. He committed himself to the cause—he visited political prisoners in jail, helped to hide people, and

36 Marshall Meyer was an American rabbi who lived in Argentina for twenty–five years. He founded the Jewish Conservative movement in Argentina and during the years of the military dictatorship, he fervently opposed repression. He visited political prisoners, obtaining the freedom of some of them, and internationally denounced the crimes of the military government. He was appointed by President Raúl Alfonsín as a member of the national commission on people who had disappeared. He received the medal of Orden del Libertador San Martín, the greatest decoration that the Argentinean government provides to foreigners.

counseled and comforted many of the mothers and fathers of "the disappeared." He did everything in his power to fight for the return of democracy. In my opinion, it was well-deserved when he was decorated by Alfonsín[37] with the Order of the Liberator San Martin, the highest honor given by Argentina. All of this happened after his having dealt with the accusations with which he was charged. I cannot opine on what actually happened because I do not know the details, but the channels for lodging a formal complaint against him existed. Judicial investigations did not reveal any offense on the part of Meyer. This just goes to show that every religious leader not only needs to act correctly in the eyes of G-d, but in the eyes of his fellow man as well. They need to go about their business with an abundance of caution in order to avoid any misunderstandings that could give rise to suspicions.

37 Ed. Note: Raúl Alfonsín was the first democratically elected president of Argentina (1983–89) after eight years of military rule; he was leader of the left leaning "Unión Cívica Radical" (Radical Civic Union).

7. ON PRAYER

SKORKA: Prayer should serve to unite people because it is a time when we are all on the same page. What is more, according to our law, prayers become more powerful if they are recited together by at least ten Jews. Prayer also serves as an act of identity. We pray using the same terms, in the same way and seeking the same results as everyone else. But beyond all that, prayer has to be an act of profound introspection, when we need to look within ourselves, find our interior life, and start a conversation with G-d. It is not an easy thing to do since we have to differentiate between our own voice and G-d's. When someone studies the Bible in depth, they do so to find guidelines that make it easier to differentiate between the two. At its core, getting closer to G-d is the goal of every mystical experience; to feel Him in some way, which is an essential interior condition for prayer. The verb "to pray" in Hebrew is "l'hitpalel," which means to judge oneself. Every time we want to get closer to G-d, the first thing we have to do is determine what our personal defects are.

BERGOGLIO: Prayer is an act of freedom, but sometimes it emerges as an attempt at control, which is the same as wanting to control God. That has to do with a deformation, with an excessive ritualism or with many other attitudes of control. Prayer is talking and listening. There are moments of profound silence, adoration, waiting to see what will happen. In prayer, there coexists this reverent silence together with a sort of haggling, like when Abraham negotiated with God for the punished citizens of Sodom and Gomorra. Moses also bargains when he pleads for his people, he hopes to convince the Lord not to punish his people. This attitude of courage goes along with humility and adoration, which are essential for prayer.

SKORKA: The worst thing that can happen to our relationship with G-d is not that we fight with Him, but that we become indifferent. A religious man, even in the worst of times, will continue talking to G-d, just as thousands of people did when they went into the gas chambers to die, shouting "Hear O Israel, The Lord is God, The Lord is One!" which is our declaration of faith. Despite everything, they continued believing in Him. For our Yom Kippur (Day of Atonement) prayer service, we have incorporated a story[38] about a document that was found in the ruins of the Warsaw Ghetto, in which the author relates that his wife and sons had died and that he is the only member of his family to have survived. He addresses G-d with a great deal of pain, yet there comes a part when he says that however much he is put to the test, he will continue to believe in Him. That is true faith.

BERGOGLIO: The indifference has many forms. When liturgical acts slide into social events, they lose force. A good example is the celebration of a marriage, which in some cases might lead someone to ask what is religious about that ceremony, because the minister preaches values, but many people are tuned in to a different frequency. They get married because they want God's blessing, but that desire seems hidden and does not become visible. In some churches–and I do not know how to cure it, honestly–in the weddings there seems to be a ferocious competition between the bridesmaids and the bride, for example with regards to the fashion or dress. These ladies do not perform any religious act; they go to show off. This weighs on my conscience. As a pastor, I am allowing it and I am

---

38 This story was written immediately after the Second World War by Zvi Kolitz. It was published in the book *Iosl Rakover habla a Dios*, Buenos Aires, Fondo de Cultura Económica, 1998.

not sure how to stop it. I give the example of weddings because it is where this issue is most evident.

SKORKA: That happens because we are living in a very secular society that is all about the here and now. The only solution that I have found for avoiding these situations is to meet the engaged couple and their parents, at which point I lay the groundwork and explain to them the value of the ceremony. I tell them not to forget that they will be entering a sanctuary, that there will not be a dress code, but there will always be enough time to put on a veil or a scarf if necessary. During that meeting, I try to dignify the wedding; to highlight what a couple's challenges will be, such as building a home and bringing children into the world. I do the same thing in my sermon. I know that it is my opportunity to make sure that the occasion does not turn into a fashion show or become focused on superficial issues.

BERGOGLIO: Continuing with the example of marriage, we also perform a marriage preparation with couples. We take a look at the reality–because some are already living together, others have only been engaged a short time–and the priest speaks with them trying to emphasize religious values. There are churches where this preparation is done very well, and in others it is more of a formality. The same is true for the first communion. For example, the girls today do not wear a first communion dress, but rather a white robe the same as all the others; the dresses have disappeared. When one wants to control prayer, when one is indifferent to the relationship with God, he ends up giving more importance to worldly things. You made reference to this culture when you spoke about the secular realm. I believe that worldliness is narcissistic, consumerist, and hedonistic. The spirit of the liturgical celebration has to have a different tone; it must be linked with the spiritual, with the encounter with God.

SKORKA: In Judaism, there is no separation between the spiritually pure and the merely material, just as there isn't a separation between body and soul. The human being is one. Everything we do with our bodies should be an expression of our deepest feelings. With regards to money, it is not a bad thing in and of itself–it depends what we do with it. It is just a means. It changes into something evil when it becomes an end in itself and the only thing that matters is a desire to have even more. Religious congregations also need money to survive and carry on with their activities. That said, although it is a necessity, they have to be extremely careful and manage it with the seriousness of a corporation or an NGO, because if they do not, they will go under. Even in the smallest synagogues, congregants pay to reserve the location of their High Holiday seats. Those that get called to the lectern to read from the Torah or the Books of the Prophets also donate money–they pay for the honor of honoring G-d with the reading. Some also pay so that someone else can have the honor of doing it; so that those who are destitute can honor G-d as well. In ancient times, when someone wanted to honor G-d, the faithful also had to take something he or she owned and present it as an offering. One of the many ways of honoring Him was by providing for material needs so that spiritual matters could be focused on. The largest donations are received during the period leading up to the Day of Atonement. The synagogue invites people of means–if and only if they are honest people as well–to give them the honor of holding the Torah. However, we do not only call on well-to-do members; we also invite those who deserve a special honor based on their personal integrity. It is necessary to maintain a balance because those that support the maintenance of the institution by donating their assets also deserve to be praised. Everyone seeks acknowledgment–some for being present throughout the year, others for their assistance with social services and others for their material support. Not everything having to do with money is bad; it depends on how it is used.

BERGOGLIO: It is interesting how we arrived at the issue of indifference and money by starting with the issue of prayer. In the Catholic Tradition, the idea of reserved places no longer works. Yes we have alms for Mass, which allows for the sustainability of worship. It is ideal that those resources, necessarily, come from the faithful and not from another place. Sometimes someone can objectify this use of money and give it a magical power; some think that thanks to a donation they might achieve who knows what, but it is not a purchase, rather it is an offering that goes along the line of what you said. I get very upset when there is a "menu of prices" for certain religious ceremonies. Two years ago, a parish in Buenos Aires had fee-based baptisms according to the day of the week. Or sometimes, when a couple wants to get married, the parish secretary meets them and gives them a "menu of prices": with a red carpet it costs this much, without the red carpet this much, and so on. That makes a business out of worship. We are the ones who cause this worldliness.

In the Gospel, Jesus formulates a very interesting reflection. He was looking together with the apostles at the donation box of the temple, and how the faithful were putting in their alms. The wealthy put in a lot of money and suddenly a widow arrived and put in a very small coin. So, Jesus said to the disciples: "This woman put in more than all of the others." He said this because the other people put in what was left over, but she put in all that she had to live on. That is the true almsgiving. It is not from what is left over, but from what causes privation. When you go to confession, I ask you if you give alms. In general, people tell me yes, so I ask them if they gaze into the eyes of those that receive it. The most common answer is "I do not know." I continue interrogating: "And do you touch the hand of the one that you offer alms, the beggar in the street?" There they turn red and do not respond. Almsgiving is a profound human generosity when it is done for a neighbor, which is the meaning of almsgiving. It is never a purchase.

SKORKA: One of the prophets' harshest criticisms of the people was that they prayed but did not act justly. You cannot do one thing and not the other–it is essential that we help our neighbors, feed the hungry and clothe the naked. Someone who has blood on his hands cannot just move on and talk to G-d. The same holds true for anyone who has robbed or stolen from someone else. We need to work toward a world in which no one has to extend his or her hand for alms–that is the real challenge. Any society in which this need exists is evidently infirm. To be sure, praying also means looking into another's eyes and touching their hands in order to understand that those who are suffering are also our brothers and that our challenge is to eradicate poverty.

BERGOGLIO: An act of justice that becomes concrete in helping one's neighbor is a prayer. If not, one falls into the sin of hypocrisy, which is like schizophrenia for the soul. One can suffer these dysfunctional features if he does not take into account that the Lord is in my brother and my brother is hungry. If a person does not take care of his brother, he cannot talk with the Father about his brother, with God. Our common tradition always took this into account. Another thing that I would like to mention is the value of repentance in prayer: to ask God to have mercy on me because I am a sinner. Jesus tells a parable[39] in which there is a rich man that is praying in the temple and he thanks the Lord because he is not like other men; he fulfills the entire law and does what is asked of him. Behind him, there is another person, a man in charge of collecting taxes to give them to the Romans. He is prostrated on the floor; without the strength to lift his head, he asks for mercy because he is a sinner. The first left exactly as he entered, but the second left justified. That is repentance, to put oneself in the presence of God, to recognize the foolishness, the sins, and to humble oneself before Him. It is because of this that the proud man is incapable of prayer, the self-sufficient man cannot pray.

SKORKA: Anyone who has sinned can come back to G-d. We should welcome whoever wants to return to the Lord. Besides, it would be good for humanity if those who have caused many to die—whether in the name of some ideology or what is even worse, in G-d's name—would perform a sincere act of contrition. The actions of these horrendous leaders come from their contemptible, religious form of hedonism; they feel as if they are greater than the Creator. They consider their orders to be irrevocable commandments that should be followed to the letter. By doing that, they do

39 Luke 18:9–14

not honor G-d, but rather illegitimate interests. These mistakes cannot be repeated. One has to learn that religion is the manifestation of the most sublime aspects of humanity, but only when it is pure. Anything else is a distortion, used to create hedonistic lives where man and his ego are idolized. The Bible is a tale of simple living and humility in which man fights to control his passions. In it we find David who makes mistakes and accepts his guilt. We see Abraham at his strongest and weakest points; we see him deal with his internal struggles; we see both his greatness and his weaknesses that come from his being human. Later on, however, people fought repeatedly for institutions, and killed in the name of G-d in order to defend them. They actually became assassins for these institutions, for the powerful or for empires. That is what has caused the weakening of the influence of religion when, in reality, what was weakened was the religious institution due to the various mistakes it made which were not based on a sincere search for G-d.

BERGOGLIO: In his moment, David was an adulterer and an intellectual assassin, but nevertheless, we venerate him as a saint because he had the courage to say "I have sinned." He humbled himself before God. One can do something horrible, but one can also realize his mistake, change his life and repair what he did. It is true that among the faithful there are those who have not only killed intellectually or physically, but also have killed indirectly through the poor use of resources by paying unjust wages. In public they may form welfare societies, but they do not pay their employees a wage corresponding to their work or they hire them "under the table." That is hypocrisy, that is the schizophrenia that I was referring to. To be certain, we know their résumés, we know that they pretend to be Catholics, but they have the indecent attitudes of those who never repent. That is why, in certain situations, I do not give communion myself; I stay back and I let the ministers give it because I do not want those people to come to me for the photo op. One could deny communion to a public sinner who has not repented, but it is very difficult to check such things. Receiving communion means receiving the body of the Lord, with the awareness that together we constitute a community. But if a man, rather than uniting the people to God, warps the lives of many people, he cannot receive communion; it would be a complete contradiction. Those cases of spiritual hypocrisy occur in many people who hide within the Church and do not live according to the justice that God proclaims. They do not show repentance either. It is what we commonly call living a double life.

8. ON GUILT

BERGOGLIO: Guilt can be understood in two senses: as a transgression and as a psychological feeling. The latter is not religious. Moreover, I would dare to say that it can even supplant a religious feeling; something like that interior voice that points out that I made a mistake, that I did something wrong. There are people who are overly scrupulous because they need to live with guilt, but that psychological feeling is unhealthy. Then coming to terms with the mercy of God is much easier while I have this feeling of guilt because I can go to confession and that's that: the Lord has forgiven me. But it is not that easy because you just want to remove the blemish; the transgression is something more serious than a mere blemish. There are people who play this guilt game and then in the encounter with the mercy of God, they transform the experience into one of going to a drycleaner, only going to clean their blemishes; and just like that they degrade things.

SKORKA: I agree 100 percent. One thing is what we hear anecdotally through folk wisdom or see in the stereotype of the guilt-inducing Jewish mother— but these things have nothing to do with the essential Judeo-Christian concept of guilt, because when one commits a sin it is possible to redeem oneself. People have to change their attitude so that they do not commit the same sin again. It is not enough to say, "I was wrong," and that is the end of the story. Of course it helps to say a prayer, or make a heartfelt charitable donation, but only when it is the result of a sincere desire for change. When people say that religions play around with the Judeo-Christian concept of relieving guilt, they show an enormous lack of understanding, because we believe that committing a sin is not the end of the world. While anyone can do the wrong thing, we do believe the situation has to be fixed and put right. But most importantly, it should not happen again.

BERGOGLIO: Guilt by itself belongs to the world of idolatry. It is just another human resource. Guilt, without atonement, does not allow us to grow.

SKORKA: I do not believe that guilt is a feeling that is solely religious—it is a cultural element as well. We reinforce feelings of guilt anytime we tell someone "Do not do this" or "Do not do that." We make children aware of the difference between right and wrong, and that is how we help them understand what it means to be guilty, a model that will drive their notions of punishment and justice. We also adhere to the idea that justice is not only something delivered by man, but that one day there will be a rendering of accounts with G-d. After all, He is the one who revealed the commandments to us—"Do not steal," "Do not murder," etc. The concept of guilt needs to exist in order for us to know that if someone does something destructive, they will have to account for their actions.

BERGOGLIO: Previously, it was very common to resort to the Bogeyman. Today, you can tell a child that the Bogeyman is coming and they will laugh in your face. But in our childhood they spoke to us about the Bogeyman. Fear is only an exaggeration, a bad method of education. The Puritan system fell into this quite a lot. The challenge is to present the offense as something that takes you away from God. Take Saint Augustine when he speaks of redemption and the love of God; referring to the sin of Adam and Eve, he calls it, "Happy fault." I take him at his word. It is as if God were to say: "I have allowed that some sin, so that their faces might fill with shame." Because then they will find the God of mercy. Otherwise, they are those Christians with good manners, but with bad habits in their hearts: the proud. Sometimes transgression makes us more humble in the presence of the Lord and brings us to ask for forgiveness.

SKORKA: Once again, we agree. Sin exists to teach us that we are not perfect. Even those who say they want to be perfect will inevitably do something wrong. They should sin just so that they realize that they cannot go it alone, so that they get frustrated occasionally regardless of how careful and well-meaning they are. Self-sufficiency destroys lives.

9. ON FUNDAMENTALISM

SKORKA: Rabbis and priests should be teachers–pointing the way, leading, trying to bring man closer to G-d. The word *rabbi* is synonymous with teacher. What is the role of the priest in Catholicism?

BERGOGLIO: It is threefold: teacher, guide of the people of God and president of the liturgical assembly, where there is a place for prayer and adoration.

SKORKA: Is your way of bringing people closer to G-d the same as ours in Judaism? We say, "I will help by teaching you what it says in the texts, but you have to want to learn."

BERGOGLIO: Part of teaching also includes this: One cannot replace another person's decision. The priest who adopts an attitude of only being a boss, like in fundamentalist groups, nullifies and emasculates those who are searching for God. The priest, in his role as teacher, instructs, proposes the truth as it is revealed, and accompanies. Though he may have to witness failure, he accompanies. The teacher who nullifies the decision-making for his disciple is not a good priest; he is a good dictator, denying others their religious personalities.

SKORKA: That is a very important point because there are Jewish communities that follow very charismatic and influential religious leaders wherein if a teacher says something should be done, there is no other alternative but to comply, even when it has to do with a person's most intimate decisions. In today's world where there is such terrible uncertainty, where everything changes from one minute to the next, many people crave something that is "true," even if it is merely superficial; something solid to hold on to in the midst of an ever-changing reality. There are certain truths with respect to G-d that we can only find by ourselves. In Judaism, as in other religions, one can find leaders that dictate how others should live, denying the religious feelings that are supposed to emanate from within each person. What goes on in Catholicism?

BERGOGLIO: The teacher presents the truth of God and shows the path. But if he is a true teacher, he allows the disciple to walk and he accompanies him in his spiritual life.

SKORKA: How many inauthentic teachers are there? Have their numbers multiplied recently?

BERGOGLIO: Yes, some small restorationist factions have continued to multiply; I call them funda-mentalists. As you said, before this heap of uncer-tainties they tell young people: "Do this, do that." So a seventeen- or eighteen-year-old boy or girl gets excited and they push them forward with rigid directives. And to be honest, they mortgage their lives and at thirty, they burst because they were not properly prepared to overcome the thousand and one crises in life, or the thousand and one shortcomings that everyone has, or the thousand and one wrongs that they are going to commit. They do not have the proper criteria to know and understand the mercy of God, for example. This type of rigid religiosity is disguised with doctrines that claim to give justifications, but in reality deprive peo-ple of their freedom and do not allow them to grow as persons. A large number end up living a double life.

SKORKA: Fundamentalism is an attitude–things are understood to be a certain way and there is noth-ing to discuss–there is no other way. We should not go to the other extreme either where things can mean anything we want them to. We have to find the middle ground. As Maimonides taught in the Middle Ages, we have to find "the golden path." It is not just a religious issue–it applies to every aspect of life beginning with politics, where there it is much more present than in religion. The trouble is that when this attitude is pres-ent in religion, it is more harmful. When people kill in the name of G-d, it is even that much more harm-ful. In a way, the damage done is also greater: because of this diabolical crime and the destruction of human dignity, the openness to faith is destroyed. To put it another way, the credibility of the faith deteriorates. I am talking about faith in a very broad sense—faith in G-d as well as faith in the creation of a world where people can live in peace and harmony.

BERGOGLIO: In general, among religions, the fundamentalists are looked at with suspicion. Therefore, the perception that the religious leader has of the fundamentalists groups in his community is very important. Some people are naïve; they do not catch on and they fall into the trap. But there is an instinct that says: "This is not the path that I want." The commandment of the Lord is: "Walk in my presence and be blameless."[40] When someone is walking, anything can happen to him, and God understands this. Part of being blameless is repentance for the mistakes we have made and the renewal that comes from the Lord. The fundamentalist cannot tolerate a fault within himself. If we are talking about a healthy religious community, it is detected immediately. You would hear: "He is an extremist, he goes too far, he needs to be a bit more understanding." Fundamentalism is not what God wants. For example, when I was a boy, in my family there was a certain Puritan tradition. It was not fundamentalist, but it had that slant. If someone close to the family divorced or separated, they could not enter

40 Genesis 17:1

your house; and they believed all Protestants were going to hell; but I remember one time I was with my grandmother, a great woman, and two women from the Salvation Army had just passed by. I was about five or six years old, and I asked her if they were nuns, because they were wearing that little hat that they used to wear. She responded to me: "No, they are Protestants, but they are good." That was the wisdom of the true religion. They were good women who did good things. That experience was contrasted with the Puritan formation that I was getting on the other hand.

SKORKA: There is a book called *G-d's Revenge* written by Gilles Kepel, a very well-known French analyst. In it, the author reviews Islamic fundamentalism, but prior to that he mentions Jewish and Christian fundamentalism. He analyzes recent political events to show how fundamentalism arises during times of crisis, such as the oil crisis of the 1970s. He then deals with the phenomenon from a sociological point of view. He finds some sort of logical explanation of the subject based on theories of group psychology. We also have cases of fundamentalism in Judaism, with the assassination of Yitzhak Rabin[41] being its most devastating symbol. We have to honor G-d through freedom and honoring oth-

41 Yitzhak Rabin was the prime minister of Israel twice. He received the Nobel Peace Prize in 1994, together with Palestinian leader Yasser Arafat, for the peace agreement both reached in Oslo. He was murdered in 1995 by a Jewish student from Israel's extreme right.

ers. G-d says we have to respect our neighbors as we do ourselves. When Jews say their daily prayers, they begin this way: "Our G-d and G-d of our fathers, G-d of Abraham, G-d of Isaac and G-d of Jacob . . ." Why do we have to repeat the name of G-d prior to each of the patriarchs? It is because each of them related to G-d in their own way. No one can arbitrarily impose "the truth" on anyone else. We should teach and guide people, after which each person will live the truth as they understand it, based on their sincere feelings. These are things that fundamentalism rejects.

BERGOGLIO: This type of restorationist fundamentalism is an opiate as well because it takes you away from the living God. Opium is an idol that alienates you, as any idol does. It reduces God to a being that you can manage with prescriptions: "If I do this everything will be fine, if I do this I will not lack anything." It is a form of buying comfort, well–being, fortune and happiness, but it leaves behind the living God, He that accompanies you along the way.

SKORKA: Fundamentalism goes even further than that; it entails evaluating and judging others. Since that person does not live the way I believe G-d says they should, I can kill them. That is the type of extreme fundamentalism that leads to hatred. And of course, what you say is correct in that it is a form of opium that alienates people. How many wealthy people go to the miracle-workers, the mystics or the cabbalists thinking that everything will be okay if they just do certain things. It occurs to me that the same thing must happen in the Catholic Church as it does in Judaism, where there are some people that donate large sums of money to rabbis for charitable work—for schools, for orphans, for rescuing kids from the street, etc., but the idea underlying all of this is that they are giving to the rabbi thinking that they then have contact with "the Man Upstairs," which will result in more profitable business dealings, as if G-d could be bought. I do not know what goes on in Catholicism . . .

BERGOGLIO: There also exists, at times, a tendency in the religious realm to pay for divine protection, to buy God, or better said, to attempt to bribe Him. God does not enter into this type of relationship. The prayer of a person with this kind of attitude is simply a soliloquy.

SKORKA: The problem is that bribery is like dancing the tango—it takes two—one to give and the other to receive. It is not just a problem with the congregant, but with the priest who takes part in it as well.

BERGOGLIO: Once, during the period of the "one-to-one,"[42] two government officials came to see me at the Flores Vicariate, saying that they had money for the shantytowns. They presented themselves as very

42 Ed. Note: *Uno a uno* (literally "one to one") was the street name given to the currency law passed in Argentina in March 1991. The law established that the Argentinean currency would always have the same value as the US dollar.

good Catholics and after a short time they offered me 400,000 pesos to improve the shantytowns. In some things I am quite naïve, but in other things I have good "alert-o-meter," and this time it worked. I started to ask them what they had in mind for the project and they finished by telling me that of the 400,000 that I would sign as having received, they were going to give me only half. I had an elegant way out: since regional vicars do not have bank accounts, and I did not either, I told them that they would have to deposit the money directly to the diocese, that they only accept donations by check or by showing a bank deposit receipt. Those men disappeared. If those people showed up uninvited with such a proposal, I presume that it is because some church member or religion had done them the favor before.

SKORKA: When all is said and done, institutions are built by men.

10. ON DEATH

BERGOGLIO: God always gives life. He gives it to you here and He will give it to you in the next life. He is the God of life, not of death. In our theological reading of evil, there is the episode of sin. Evil entered the world through the cunning of the Devil that–as we have already said–became jealous because God made man as the most perfect being. It is because of this that the Devil entered into the world. In our faith, death is a consequence of human freedom. We were, by our sins, those who opted for death, which entered into the world because we made room for disobedience to the plan of God. Sin entered as pride before God's plan, and with it, death.

SKORKA: In Judaism, there is a whole range of explanations for death. We do not have the concept of original sin; instead, we interpret the situation in the following way. There were two trees in the midst of Eden, one was the Tree of Knowledge of Good and Evil and the other was the Tree of Life. Basically, they were regular trees. The Tree of Knowledge of Good and Evil was not, as is often said, an apple tree; it was more likely a fig tree, and Adam and Eve wound up making clothing for themselves with its leaves.[43] The same tree that prompted the transgression against the divine commandments also served to cover them.[44] These were simple trees; they were reminders of what should not be done and that man does not control everything. But man challenged G-d. There are a myriad of possible interpretations regarding that sin–it is not an issue of dogma. Something was lost, but it is not all that clear exactly what. Some part of man's spirituality died, but death had already been established as part of nature. I believe that at the time G-d created man, He determined that people would have finite lives. Perhaps there is something positive about death. Everything that G-d made, He made for the good of the world. Death is not an easy topic. Paradoxically, it is life's greatest mystery and we define what we do with our journey here on Earth based on how we resolve it. If we believe that absolutely everything comes to an end with death–that as the verse says, we return to dust[45]–we are not go-

43 Genesis 3:7
44 Based on Berajot 40, a
45 Genesis 3:19

78

ing to struggle in search of transcendence; instead we will focus on the here and now by living a hedonistic, self-centered and egotistical lifestyle. Man, however, is actually similar to a tree. He must complete a cycle–giving of his fruit and afterwards letting new cycles emerge from the seeds that he plants himself. What life proves to us is that there is some kind of transcendence here in this world. The biblical text makes insinuations; it does not say precisely what happens to someone when they die. However, it does emphasize transcendence–that what we do today will have an effect on our children. Throughout religious literature there are stories about curses that pass from parents to children or from one family to another. There is the example of Eli, the High Priest who took in and then taught Samuel. Since Eli's own sons did not behave properly and he did not reprimand them, a curse was placed on his family that was passed on to succeeding generations. Jeremiah was the last one that we know of who got stuck with this curse. The prophet did not marry, did not have children and did not build a home. As he said himself, he was a man of contention and strife;[46] the one who prophesied about the destruction of Jerusalem. It is all pain and suffering. Since the Bible is quite implicit about this, in Judaism we have an official interpretation–the Talmud–in which the idea of the world to come is presented explicitly. The idea

46 Jeremiah 15:10

that there is a hell and a heavenly place called Eden also comes up. Where did all this start? I believe that it was when the sages asked themselves why it is that the righteous suffer. Where is G-d's justice then? Why were the sages who wanted to teach Torah all martyred and stoned to death by the Romans during Hadrian's rule? Why did G-d allow it? The answer is that there is another life and we are rewarded there for everything that we have done down here on Earth. That other life is a matter of intuition and faith that comes from very deeply felt religious experiences. For those of us who believe that to be human is sublime, including agnostics, death is not just the dissolution of the id, but is a challenge to leave an inheritance for our children, our students and all those around us. As opposed to a material inheritance, it is a matter of spirituality and values.

BERGOGLIO: I want to return to the topic of inheritance. To think that we have to leave an inheritance is an extremely serious anthropological and religious concept that speaks about dignity. It is to say to oneself: I do not want to close in on myself, I do not want to fence in my life, what is mine will at least be passed on to my children, to those to whom I will leave my inheritance, and even though one might not have children, the inheritance still exists. This is very present in the Bible. It is the example of the vineyard of Naboth[47]:

47 1 Kings 21

the son receives it and is not going to sell it, but rather he conserves it and also passes it on to future generations. The person who lives only in the moment, does not contemplate the issue of inheritance; the only important thing to him is the moment, the years of life that he is able to have. Inheritance, on the other hand, is developed over time through the pilgrimage of humanity: man receives something and has to leave behind something better. When one is young, he does not so much look toward the end, he values much more the moment, but I remember two rhymes from my grandmother: "See that God watches you, see that He is watching you; see that you will have to die and you do not know when."[48] She had that saying under the glass top of her little nightstand, and each time that she went to bed she would read it. After seventy years I still have not forgotten it. There is another rhyme that she told me that she had read at an Italian cemetery: "Man who walks, stop and think about your pace, your steps, the final step." She impressed on me the awareness that everything must end, that everything has to be left behind in good order. With respect to the Christian life, death has to accompany you on the way. In my case, for example, I think every day that I am going to

48 Ed. Note: The original in Spanish: "Mira que te mira Dios, mira que te está mirando, mira que te has de morir y no sabes cuándo."

die. This does not distress me, because the Lord and life itself have given me the proper preparation. I saw my ancestors die and now it is my turn. When? I do not know. In the Christian tradition, during the days of Easter, we read a passage in Latin that admirably states that life and death fight hand to hand. This happens in each one of us and it is not only a reference to biological terms, but rather to the way that one lives and dies. In the Gospels the topic of the Last Judgment appears, and it is linked in one way or another with love. Jesus says: To my right shall be all those who helped their neighbor, and to my left, all those that did not, because what you did to one of these, you did to me.[49] For Christians, one's neighbor is the person of Christ.

SKORKA: What you said about the internal struggle between life and death is really interesting to me. It reminds me of the expressions "life instinct" and "death instinct," which in reality Freud did not really discover by himself. They appear in several verses of Deuteronomy[50] in which Moses tells the people of Israel that G-d has called heaven and earth as witnesses against them—that life and death have placed blessings and curses before them, and that they should choose life. That internal struggle is real—there are people who

49 Matthew 25:31-46
50 30:19-20

are dead inside even though they are still alive. I am reminded of Florencio Sanchez,[51] the playwright who had one of his characters say that a man who has no personality is a dead man walking. Death is a very profound concept; there are spiritual suicides and slow suicides like that of an addicted smoker. There are the people who drag race in the streets, who show a complete disregard for other people's lives as well as their own. Theirs is a constant flirtation with death. We have to ask ourselves, what do we do about death and the daily toll of anguish it causes? I deal with the anguish of death through my faith; I believe that when it does happen to me, I will then exist in some other reality of a spiritual nature. We believe that there is another life after death, but it would be arrogant for us to talk as if we knew everything about that world to come when we can barely describe it.

BERGOGLIO: Generally the word *believe* is used and linked to the term *opinion*, but here we use it with another meaning, with the meaning of resolve, of adherence. When I say, "I believe that there is a hereafter," in reality I am saying that I am sure of it. In theological language, to believe is a certainty, and eternal life takes shape here; in the experience of the encounter with God, it begins in the amazement of the en-

---

51 In his novel *Los Muertos*, the character Lisandro expresses these sentiments.

counter. Moses meets God when he is eighty years old, having already grown a belly; he tended his father-in-law's sheep and all of a sudden, a burning bush, astonishment. He says, "I have seen God." In other parts of the Bible, for example, in the Book of Judges,[52] there is a fear of death after having seen God. Seeing God is not understood as a punishment, but rather it is the experience of entering into another dimension and knowing that one is headed there. This is the richest interpretation that I find in the Bible with regard to the afterlife. You cannot live in a state of awe permanently, but the memory of that moment is never forgotten. We believe that there is another life because we have already begun to feel it here. It is not a mellow feeling, but rather something astonishing through which God has revealed Himself to us.

SKORKA: There are a lot people who do not possess that sense of awe that you mentioned. I would call them agnostic; nevertheless they also treat death matter-of-factly. Of course they always say they do not want to suffer and do not want to be in any great pain when they die, but they do not worry about it. They say, "When it is my turn, it is my turn." That is why I do not believe the theory that belief in a world to come is a theological invention for mitigating anxiety brought on by the thought of dying. That kind of anguish can be caused by any number of things, such as the fear

52 Judges 13:22

84

that everyone has of the unknown. Even if we knew for sure that there is a world to come, we would still be scared because we do not know what it is. Any change in our lives is stressful. Life provides us with some experiences that cannot be explained simply or easily but convey a very subtle message. I remember studying the books of the prophets as a teenager. I felt as one with them and understood their conversations with G-d. I had a unique sensibility, a family tradition passed down by people I never knew who died in the Holocaust. Those people were very spiritual—even more so than my parents and grandparents. Why did I have that sensibility? How did that come to be written in my genes? It is something that goes deeper than my conscious or subconscious. It means that there are other dimensions—and a different life.

BERGOGLIO: If belief in the afterlife were a psychological mechanism to avoid anguish, it would not help us. The anguish would come anyway. Death is a tearing away; that is why we live with anguish. One is attached and does not want to go; he is afraid. There is nothing you can imagine beyond this life that can free you from that. Even the most faithful feel that they are being stripped of something, that they have to leave behind part of their existence, their story. These are untransferable feelings. Perhaps those that have been in a coma have perceived something like this. In the Gospels, Jesus himself, before the prayer on the Mount of Olives, says that his soul is anguished to the point of death.[53] It is written that He is afraid of what is to come. According to the Gospel accounts, he dies reciting Psalm 22: "My God, my God, why have you abandoned me."[54] From this no one is exempt. I trust in the mercy of God, that He will be benevolent. Let us say: there is no anesthesia for anguish, but there is the capacity to bear it.

SKORKA: It is very stressful to know that one's time is limited and even more so not knowing where the limit is. It would be terrible to think that our life is nothing more than a meaningless accident of nature and that everything ends inexorably in death. If that were the case, our lives would have no meaning; much less our sense of values or justice . . . anyway, that would be an extreme point of view. Two possibilities remain. For those who do not want to bother with the issue of G-d, human life has an intrinsic meaning–its message of generosity and justice passed on from generation to generation. And for those of us who do have faith in G-d, obviously we believe that His spark lies within us and that death is nothing more than a change in our situation.

BERGOGLIO: A short time ago I read a writer from the second century who imagined Easter as a path in its entirety, and he applied it to this life. Somehow he

---

53 Matthew 26:38
54 Psalms 22:2

said: "Do not lose sight of where you are going, do not make the journey too entertaining, because then you may get carried away and forget the goal." We have to take on the responsibility of our journey; in it will appear in all of our creativity, and our work to transform this world, but we must not forget that we are on a path toward a promise. To journey is the creative responsibility to fulfill the command of God: to grow, be fruitful and subdue the earth. The first Christians were united around the image of death with hope, and they used as a symbol the anchor. So, hope was the anchor that one had dug into the shore, and they held on to the rope in order to advance without losing their way. Salvation is in hope, that it will be fully revealed to us, but in the meantime we are holding on to the rope and doing what we believe that we have to do. Saint Paul tells us: "In hope we are saved."

SKORKA: Even though the Latin word also means "to wait"—*to hope* does not mean taking a passive approach with respect to our goals. One can be proactive as well. The Jewish people lived for two thousand years with the hope of returning to their land, and for a long time, that hope was reduced to praying to G-d. But there came a point when many Jews decided to leave Europe and went to live in Israel. That is the difference between hope and optimism, which is not a goal in itself, but is a way of looking at life.

BERGOGLIO: Optimism is a more psychological

issue, an attitude toward life. There are people who always see the glass half full and others, on the contrary, who see the glass half empty. Hope, at its base, has something passive about it because it is a gift from God. The virtue of hope cannot be acquired by ourselves; it has to be given by the Lord. How you use it, how you administer it, how to assume it is a different thing ... In our understanding, hope is one of the three theological virtues, together with faith and charity. We tend to give more importance to faith and charity. Nevertheless, hope is the one that frames the structure of the entire path. The danger is to fall in love with the path and lose the vision of the goal; and another danger is quietism: to be looking at the goal and not to do anything on the way. Christianity had very strong periods of quietist movements that went against the command of God, which says that one has to work and transform the earth.

SKORKA: Those who are imbued with a deep sense of faith face death in a different, calmer way. A man I knew from my congregation comes to mind. He was a Jew who was full of faith. One day his daughter called me to ask if I could go to see him because he was in bad shape and the doctor had told him that his days were numbered. Obviously, I said I would go. I went and figured that I would find a man on death's doorstep. Instead, the man was completely aware of his surroundings—no one would have guessed that he was about to die. I spoke with him as if he were a completely healthy man. However, since his daughter told me that he was terminally ill, I wanted to be very careful around him, so I said goodbye to him in a special way. In Hebrew, I told him, "Stay at peace." He extended his hand to me and said, "Okay my dear rabbi, we will see each other soon in the world to come." This man had enormous faith and was completely at peace. He said goodbye to this life, with life. He passed away two days later.

BERGOGLIO: But anguish exists. It is the moment of detachment, of separation. When one is getting closer, one feels it. Detachment is not easy, but I believe that God is there ready to take your hand when you are about to leap. One has to abandon himself in the hands of the Lord; alone, one cannot survive.

SKORKA: A young man who is forced to confront death thinks about everything he did not get to do with his life. In anguish he cries, "I did not get to do what I wanted!" Many of his dreams will remain unrealized. "What kind of career would I have had?" "What kind of father would I have been?" Over time as we pass through the various stages of our existence, we start to deal with thoughts of death differently–it will always be distressing to think about–but different. Jewish mysticism talks about the soul, which remains for a time at the place of our death. It does not go directly to the heavens. This speaks to our anguish at the time of death and the difficulty of separating ourselves from this life. There are people who seem to find a certain peace moments before–their anxiety is reduced by the idea that they are giving themselves over. It is not that the story is over, but instead they are giving themselves over to Someone.

11. ON EUTHANASIA

SKORKA: Without a doubt, we have to support the medical sciences so that people can live better. But be careful! In no way should we support futile medical care. Artificially extending someone's life by hooking them up to machines for the sole purpose of sustaining their heartbeat and breathing does not make the least bit of sense. It just creates added stress for the family members keeping vigil over terminally ill loved ones. Yes, we should prolong life, but only for those who are fully alive.

BERGOGLIO: Our morality also says that one has to do what is necessary and ordinary, in those cases where the end is foreseeable. Quality of life must be ensured. The strength of medicine, in terminal cases, is not so much about making someone live another three days or two months, but rather in making sure the body suffers as little as possible. You are not obligated to conserve life with extraordinary methods. That can go against the dignity of the person. But active euthanasia is different; that is killing. I believe that today there is covert euthanasia: our social security pays up until a certain amount of treatment and then says "may God help you." The elderly are not taken care of like they should be, but rather they are treated as discarded material. Sometimes they are deprived of medicine and ordinary care, and that is what is killing them.

SKORKA: We clearly agree that we should not allow any procedure that is an affront to human dignity. Euthanasia is a very difficult subject because there are people who are really living in horrendous conditions and are looking for whatever way they can to cut their life short. Active euthanasia sends a message that we are the sole owners of our bodies and our lives; for that same reason we do not approve of it. We believe that G-d is still the master of our existence, regardless of the fact that He gave us free will. When someone commits suicide, at that moment they are saying that their whole being belongs to themselves; that they are the ones who decide matters of life and death. It is a serious rejection of G-d.

BERGOGLIO: There was a time when they did not perform funerals for those that committed suicide because they had not continued on toward the goal; they ended the path when they wanted to. But I still respect the one who commits suicide; he is a person who could not overcome the contradictions in his life. I do not reject him. I place him in the merciful hands of God.

SKORKA: In Judaism there are two points of view with respect to suicide. The first teaches that someone who commits suicide should be buried in a separate place and we omit certain prayers that are customarily recited in memory of the deceased. The other view is that perhaps people who kill themselves, at the very last moment, after they have already "pulled the trigger," repent for what they have done. They should be judged as if in their final moment they had committed an involuntary act, which is something that does not get punished. Another way to look at it is that it is a contagious disease that condemned them to death. Each time I have had to deal with a suicide, my explanation to the family was that the deceased had an illness, that they were very confused and had no idea what they were doing. It is the worst possible effect of depression that results from a chemical imbalance in both the body and the mind. They feel that they need to depart from this life; that they cannot go on living. When people ask me brokenheartedly, "Did I mean so little to him or her that they decided to leave me forever?" I try to restore their loved one's status and good name.

BERGOGLIO: I like this interpretation of the sickness. There arrives a moment when someone cannot take responsibility for every decision that they make. I prefer to interpret suicide like this, and not as an act of pride, but I would like to go back to euthanasia; I am convinced that now we are seeing covert euthanasia. The patient must be given everything necessary and ordinary to be able to live while there is hope for life. In terminal cases, it is not obligatory to do the extraordinary. Moreover, even though there is life expectancy, extraordinary measures, for example, the insertion of a breathing tube to give someone a few more days of life, are not obligatory.

SKORKA: Speaking from the Talmud, I would say that using extraordinary measures means not letting someone die. If there is something, anything, that can keep them alive–do not stop it. But if we know that a patient does not have any cerebral activity, and a strict protocol has been followed to ensure that there are not any vital signs, they should slowly, very carefully, start turning off the machines. I am totally against futile efforts at life support. The rules that make up Jewish law, the *Halacha*, say that it is allowable to remove anything that is used to keep someone alive if they would otherwise die without it. That is to say that if the placement of a pillow under someone's head is the only thing preventing someone from dying, then take it away. If it is salt under their tongue, take it away. Debating futile life support is something totally different than active euthanasia. When there is nothing that can be done, it is not right to keep pumping drugs into someone to

94

artificially keep them alive. I respect profoundly those who tell me that they really can do something that will allow patients to maintain a full life, at which point everything should be done. However, if they are sure that there is no chance of survival, they need to let the patient live peacefully during the time they have left. We are talking about the advanced stages of a disease, when all the doctors say it is terminal. If a dying person has no chance of recovering, it does not make sense to do a blood transfusion or hook them up to a respirator just to prolong their life for another twenty–four hours. If someone is suffering they should be given painkillers and drugs that will make them as comfortable as possible, but no more than that. We do not respect life by keeping patients in agony.

BERGOGLIO: In Catholic morality, no one is obligated to use extraordinary measures to cure others. It is not about clinging to a life when one knows that it is not alive any more. While there is the possibility of reversing the illness, everything possible should be done; but the extraordinary methods should be used only if there is hope of recuperation.

12. ON THE ELDERLY

SKORKA: Old age has never been easy. I will start off with the scene in the Bible where Jacob tells Pharaoh that he has lived a short, difficult 130 years.[55] Old age is problematic because instead of looking toward the future, we begin to look back at the past. Still, it can be a wonderful time in our lives if we have really lived fully and with intensity, because by then we will have come to understand the meaning of life. However, today old age is something we worry about because in the present culture the elderly are treated as disposable material. Modern life, instead of allowing people a little more time to relax, has got them running faster and faster. It is not just a matter of material wealth; going to the gym, traveling and other activities have

55 Genesis 47:9

become practically obligatory. There is just no time to take care of the elderly. For us to get a better sense of things, it is important that we try to visualize how the elderly live in solitude; whether it is because their friends are no longer around, or because the generational gap between them and their children makes it difficult for them to have a conversation. The elderly are not just things; they are human beings that deserve our care. Whenever we visit any of the countless old age homes throughout the city of Buenos Aires, we have to ask ourselves, "Are these decent living conditions?" Today the elderly are pushed aside. There is a biblical verse–"You shall rise up before a graying head, and honor the face of an old man."[56] Life is a struggle and it is very hard when those who have fought with dignity spend their final years terribly alone. Sometimes, homes for the aged are top notch when it comes to medical treatment, but from a spiritual point of view they leave a lot to be desired . . . the elderly need love, affection and conversation.

BERGOGLIO: I would like to reiterate what you said about disposing. Before, we were able to speak of the oppressors and the oppressed in our society. Over time, we discovered that such a category is not sufficient, that it needed to have something else added: the included and the excluded. Today things are much more savage and we have to add another

56 Leviticus 19:32

contradiction: those that fit in and those that are left over. In this consumerist, hedonist and narcissistic society, we are accustomed to the idea that there are people that are disposable, and among them there is a special place for the elderly. Parents work, and they have to resort to a nursing home to take care of the grandparents, but many times it is not an issue of being busy at work, but mere egoism: the elderly are bothersome in the house, they smell bad. They end up being stored away in a nursing home like an overcoat that is hung up in the closet during the summer. There are families in which there is no other option, but every weekend they visit their grandparents or they bring them to their own homes; they are cared for amidst their loved ones. This is not disposing; on the contrary, it is a very costly reality. But in many cases, when I visit nursing homes, I ask the elderly about their children and they answer that they are not going to see them because they have to work; they try to cover for them. There are many who abandon those that fed them, who educated them, who wiped their bottoms. It hurts me; it makes me weep inside. We will not speak about what I call covert euthanasia: the poor attention to the elderly in hospitals and in health insurance that does not give them the medicine and attention they need. The elderly are transmitters of a story, they bring us memories, the memories of a people, of a nation, of a family, of a culture, of a religion . . . They have lived through so much and even if some of them were annoying, they deserve serious consideration. It always strikes me that the fourth commandment is the only one that carries with it a promise: "Honor your father and your mother and you will have a long life on earth." In the way that you received them with honor, God is going to bless you in your old age. This shows us the mentality of God toward old age. God must be very fond of the old because those who are pious with their parents are showered with blessings. At seventy-four years of age, I am beginning old age and I will not resist it. I am prepared and I would like to be like a vintage wine, not one gone sour. The bitterness of an old person is worse than anything else, because there is no turning back. The elderly are called to peace and tranquility. I ask for that grace for myself.

SKORKA: Like you said, you have to be prepared for every stage of your life, including old age. Learning to live as an older person is often very difficult from a spiritual standpoint because some people are not ready when the time comes, so they let all of their life's frustrations and prejudices grow and fester. When we are children, we have a father and mother that set examples for us and try to provide an education and a model for how we should live. There comes a certain time when it is important to realize that our mother and father have changed. It is wonderful to have parents that maintain their intellectual edge in their old age because then you can maintain a dialogue. I remember my father as having been much wiser when he was older than at any other time in his life. The way in which he left this life was a lesson in dignity for me, but it does not always happen that way. Sometimes people withdraw and society's great challenge is to know how to deal with those situations so that we are present and can maintain caring relationships. If honoring our parents were easy, there would be no need for a divine commandment. Our emerging throwaway society has caused the elderly to surrender due to our neglecting them. When I say surrender, I am referring to anyone that gives up on life, either by euthanasia or their own withdrawal.

BERGOGLIO: Deuteronomy Chapter 26 has always impressed me; my soul benefited a lot from the section that says: "When you will arrive in the land that God will give to your parents, and when you will dwell in houses that you did not construct and when you will eat fruit from trees that you did not plant . . ." It continues listing many things that one did not make, but nevertheless possesses. To look at the elderly is to recognize that that man made his path of life toward me. There is a whole plan of God walking with this person and it started with his ancestors and it continues with his children. When we believe that history starts with us, we stop honoring the elderly. Often, when I am a little down, one of the texts that I run to is this chapter from Deuteronomy, to realize that I am just one more link, that I have to honor those that have preceded me and that I have to allow myself to be honored by those that are going to follow, to those to whom I have to transmit the inheritance. That is one of the strongest actions of old age. The old man knows, consciously or unconsciously, that he has to leave behind a testament of life; he does not make it explicit, but he lives like that. I was lucky to know my four grandparents; when the first one died I was sixteen years old. All of them gave me something and I remember them all well and distinctly. The wisdom of the elderly has helped me a lot and it is because of this that, time and again, I tend to venerate them.

13. ON WOMEN

BERGOGLIO: In Catholicism, for example, many women lead a liturgy of the word, but do not exercise the priesthood, because in Christianity the High Priest is Jesus, a male. In the theologically grounded tradition the priesthood passes through man. The woman has another function in Christianity, reflected in the figure of Mary. It is the figure that embraces society, the figure that contains it, the mother of the community. The woman has the gift of maternity, of tenderness; if all these riches are not integrated, a religious community not only transforms into a chauvinist society, but also into one that is austere, hard and hardly sacred. The fact that a woman cannot exercise the priesthood does not make her less than the male. Moreover, in our understanding, the Virgin Mary is greater than the apostles. According to a monk from the second century, there are three feminine dimensions among Christians: Mary as Mother of the Lord, the Church and the Soul. The feminine presence in the Church has not been emphasized much, because the temptation of chauvinism has not allowed for the place that belongs to the women of the community to be made very visible.

SKORKA: Christianity adopted the priest's role from the Hebrew Bible, wherein the priesthood is patrilineal. However, matrilineal descent determines whether someone is Jewish–if the mother is Jewish, the child is Jewish. Based on our beliefs, the priestly rites also used to be performed by men. Today however, we have teachers[57] instead of priests. Because of that, a woman with knowledge of the Torah can teach others and respond to questions about how to act in accordance with Jewish law.

BERGOGLIO: Catholics, when we speak of the Church, we do so in feminine terms. Christ is betrothed to the Church, a woman. The place where it receives the most attacks, where it receives the most punches, is always the most important. The enemy of human nature–Satan–hits hardest where there is more salvation, more transmission of life, and the woman–as an existential place–has proven to be the most attacked in history. She has been the object of use, of profit, of slavery, and was relegated to the background; but in

57 The word *rabbi* means "teacher."

the Scriptures we have cases of heroic women that have transmitted to us what God thinks about them, like Ruth, Judith . . . What I would like to add is that feminism, as a unique philosophy, does not do any favors to those that it claims to represent, for it puts women on the level of a vindictive battle, and a woman is much more than that. The feminist campaign of the '20s achieved what they wanted and it is over, but a constant feminist philosophy does not give women the dignity that they deserve. As a caricature, I would say that it runs the risk of becoming chauvinism with skirts.

SKORKA: Within the traditionalist (Masorti) movement, women's religious role has changed. Rabbinical seminaries around the world grant women the title of Rabbi. The truth is that from a historical point of view, the law contains no direct prohibition against women teaching Torah, nor is there any real reason to deny them the title of Rabbi. When we look at the role and portrayals of women in both biblical and Talmudic literature, there are many attributes that correspond to what you just said. The Talmud contains the Marriage Contract, whose original idea was that the woman–we are talking more than two thousand years ago–would have a document that would prevent the man from divorcing her easily. That is to say that to do it would entail a great economic hardship on the man, making it a question of practicality. What was the point? It was to safeguard the woman and ensure that she lives with dignity.

Throughout the Jewish people's historical wanderings, there have been moments of spectacular greatness with respect to the consideration given to women. The Bible provides us with some great examples. David's story to take one: he was the descendant of two women, Tamar and Ruth, who had enormous willpower and tremendous spirituality. However, there are other times when, for various reasons, there have been Jewish movements that have not treated women with generosity and respect, making them second class citizens. Why? We lived firmly entwined with other nations and male chauvinism was a constant feature throughout human history. There have been many cultures where men held more power than women and the Jewish people were not immune to these influences or committing vile acts of their own.

On the other hand, I think it deserves mentioning that in the most observant Jewish communities they adopt rules regarding modesty that prevent a man from holding hands with, or kissing, a woman who is not his wife. The women are also required to wear wigs, clothes that cover most of the body, etc. These rules have to do with tempering instinctive temptations. In an Orthodox synagogue, the women are upstairs and they do not pray together with the men. There is a separate place for them. Everyone has their own opinion regarding this issue. I believe that we all have to struggle with ourselves to try and repress our natural instincts. It is fine that there are those who feel that dressing and acting modestly helps them to conduct themselves with dignity. The risk is that this way of dealing with things may be used as camouflage to cover up disordered attitudes. Personally, I believe that the desire to live modestly is something that comes from serious introspection. I think that when either a man or a woman is going through a very hard time and asks for or receives a strong hug or kiss from someone of the opposite sex, it is an act of kindness that begins and ends with that particular situation.

14. ON ABORTION

BERGOGLIO: The moral problem with abortion is of a pre-religious nature because the genetic code of the person is present at the moment of conception. There is already a human being. I separate the issue of abortion from any religious concept. It is a scientific problem. To not allow further progress in the development of a being that already has the entire genetic code of a human being is not ethical. The right to life is the first human right. Abortion is killing someone that cannot defend himself.

SKORKA: The problem with our society is that we have lost a great deal of our respect for the sanctity of life. Problem number one is that we talk about abortion as if it were no big deal and the most normal thing in the world. It is not. Even if it is only a cell, we are still talking about a human being. Therefore, the issue merits a very special forum for discussion. What we often find is that everyone has an opinion, even though they are misinformed, or have no knowledge of the subject.

In general, Judaism condemns it, but there are situations where it is permitted; when the mother's life is in danger, for example. Abortion is allowed in various circumstances. What is interesting is that in analyzing the *Law of Nations*, what would become *jus gentium* in the Talmud, the ancient Jewish sages ruled that it should be absolutely prohibited in other societies. My interpretation is that since they knew what was being done in Rome, they wanted to avoid a discussion of abortion where Jews were living in a society with such little respect for life. In the Talmud one can find an exhaustive analysis on the topic of the death penalty. Even though the punishment appears in the Torah, there are sages who opined that its use should be so restricted that it would never actually be carried out. There are also those who argued for a less restrictive policy. Depending on the particular situation they are faced with at the time, the sages of each new generation will decide the criteria for which the penalty is applied.

The history regarding abortion is similar. Of course Judaism rejects and condemns it, with the exception of when the mother is clearly in danger of dying as explained in the Mishnah. In those cases, her life comes first. Other cases based on rape, serious birth defects, etc., are topics that have been debated by the rabbis of every generation. There are positions that are more restrictive and others that are less restrictive. The factor of holiness—understood as a supreme respect and consideration for human life in all its forms—is fundamental and should be the foundation and starting point from which we analyze and discuss this issue.

15. ON DIVORCE

BERGOGLIO: The issue of divorce is different from the marriage between people of the same sex. The Church always condemns the Divorce Law, but it is true that there are different anthropological records in this case. In the 1980s, it was a much more religious debate, because marriage until death is a very strong value in Catholicism. Nevertheless, today Catholic Doctrine reminds its divorced members who have remarried that they are not excommunicated–even though they live in a situation on the margin of what indissolubility of marriage and the sacrament of marriage require of them–and they are asked to integrate into the parish life. The Orthodox Churches have an even greater openness with respect to divorce. In that debate there was opposition, but with nuances. There were extreme positions that not everybody supported.

Some said that it was better that they did not approve of divorce, but there were also others, who were open to a dialogue from a political standpoint.

SKORKA: In the Jewish religion, the institution of divorce exists and rules are applied based on *Halacha*, the rabbinical law. Needless to say, it is a big deal. It is not a matter of faith, as it is in Catholicism, where its position comes from the reading of the Gospels that say that Jesus took a very hard line on divorce, similar to that adopted by the house of Shammai as the Talmud attests. In Judaism, when the marriage is not working out, the couple is assisted in formalizing an act of divorce only after a serious effort has been put into reconciling the two parties of their differences. I present the issue in those terms because in Judaism neither rabbis nor rabbinical courts "declare" or "decree" the new status of the parties, they only supervise the dissolution so that it is done according to the rules. The man and the woman declare and assume their new status, just as they did when they were married. It is a private action performed by those two people, under the supervision of someone knowledgeable in the law to make sure it is done correctly. That is why there has not been much conflict for us in the aforementioned debate. A similar situation occurred during the debate regarding assisted reproduction. Judaism is in favor of it because it is a way to help G-d so that a woman can become a mother, easing that person's suffering. It is a more fluid position than that of Catholicism.

Catholicism has stronger and more restrictive positions on these topics. However, when we pose these questions in the midst of a democratic society, we have to try to arrive at a consensus. The first principle needs to be that life is sacred; we cannot just play with cells as if they were clay–something that is taught in Christianity as well as Judaism. Both the religious and those who take a more liberal position have to come to an agreement–each side has to cede something. However, we can only give ground up to a point because life is sacred. Each side will have its own interpretation of what that means, but with a mutual understanding that life deserves the utmost respect. If we do not agree on that, we cannot move forward.

16. ON SAME–SEX MARRIAGE

SKORKA: I believe that the way the topic of gay marriage was treated in the past lacked the depth of analysis that it deserves. While it is true that there are already many same-sex couples who live together and deserve a legal solution to issues such as retirement benefits, inheritances, etc.,it would be best for them if a new legal status were created. However, to equate a homosexual couple with a heterosexual couple is something else entirely. It is not just a matter of beliefs, but of being conscious that we are talking about one of the building blocks that form the foundation of our society. There is still a lack of analysis and anthropological study regarding this topic. At the same time, of course, we should have given more space for the various religions to provide information since they are the carriers and shapers of our culture. There should have been organized debates at the heart of each faith, incorporating each of their various sects in order to form a complete range of opinions.

BERGOGLIO: Religion has a right to give an opinion as long as it is in service to the people. If someone asks my advice, I have the right to give it to them. The religious minster, at times, draws attention to certain points of private or public life because he is the parishioners' guide. However, he does not have the right to force anything on anyone's private life. If God, in creation, ran the risk of making us free, who am I to get involved? We condemn spiritual harassment that takes place when a minister imposes directives, conduct, and demands in such a way that it takes away the freedom of the other person. God left the freedom to sin in our hands. One has to speak very clearly about values, limits, commandments, but spiritual and pastoral harassment is not allowed.

SKORKA: Judaism has many different branches. The extremely Orthodox have an excessive number of rules–they demand that their followers live a certain way. The leader of the community says "this is the way it is" and there is no room for discussion, so in the end they meddle in people's lives. On the other hand, the rabbis in the other branches perform their roles solely in their capacity as teachers, which is not invasive. I might say, "The law says this, try to do the right thing according to the tradition," but that is all. There is a debate in the Talmud[58] about whether we should impose the right way of doing things or just try to convince people to follow them. I think that we should convince and not be invasive according to the following model– the parent who acts correctly and sets an example for their child. Paradoxically, it is also a way that beliefs are imposed, but through teaching and not through force or coercion.

Getting back to the topic at hand, Judaism prohibits sexual relations between two men. The exact words that the Bible uses are that men should not have relations together in the same way that men have them with women. That is the basis for any position taken on this issue. Since Genesis, the human ideal is the union of a man and a woman. Jewish law is clear–homosexuality is not allowed. On the other hand, I respect everyone as long as they are modest and keep their private lives to themselves. With respect to the new law, it does not make sense to me from an anthropological point of view. Upon re-reading Freud and Levi-Strauss, when they refer to the basic elements of what we call culture and the overriding importance they place on sexual ethics and the prohibition against incestuous relationships as part of the process of civilization–I worry about what will result from these changes to the core values of our society.

58 Shabbat 88, a

BERGOGLIO: I have the same exact opinion; in order to define it I would use the expression "anthropologic regression," a weakening of the institution that is thousands of years old and that was forged according to nature and anthropology. Fifty years ago, concubinage, or co-habitation, was not very socially common like it is now. It was even a clearly derogatory word. Later, the whole thing changed. Today, living together before getting married, even though it is not right from a religious point of view, does not have the same negative connotation in society that it had fifty years ago. It is a sociological fact that co-habitation certainly does not have the fullness, or the greatness of marriage, which has thousands of years of value that deserves to be defended. It is because of this that we warn about its possible devaluation and, before modifying the law, one must reflect a lot about all that it will put in play.

For us, what you just pointed out is also important, the foundation of Natural Law that appears in the Bible that speaks about the union between man and woman. There have always been homosexuals. The island of Lesbos was known because homosexual women lived there, but it never occurred historically that they would seek to give them the same status of marriage. They were tolerated or they were not, they were admired or they were not, but they were never put on the same level. We know that in times of momentous change the homosexual phenomenon grew, but in this period, it is the first time that the legal problem of assimilating it to marriage has arisen, and this I consider an anti-value and an anthropological regression. I say this because it transcends the religious issue, it is anthropological. If there is a union of a private nature, there is neither a third party nor is society affected. Now, if the union is given the category of marriage and they are given adoption rights, there could be children affected. Every person needs a male father and a female mother that can help them shape their identity.

SKORKA: When they modified the law to separate civil and religious marriage during the presidency of Raúl Alfonsín, I believed they did the right thing. Before that, in order to marry a couple, we had to have the civil marriage certificate in hand. It did not make sense to me that in a democratic society there should be a connection between the civil and religious ceremonies. I prefer that these two worlds do not mix. Nevertheless, when referring to laws that deal with such sensitive issues on a human level, there should be more strenuous debate among the different faiths and we should delve further into the subject than we have in the past.

BERGOGLIO: I insist that our opinion about the marriage between two people of the same sex is not based on religion, but rather on anthropology. When the head of the Government of the City of Buenos Aires, Mauricio Macri, did not appeal the judge's opinion right away authorizing a [same-sex] wedding, I felt that I had something to say, to inform; I saw myself with an obligation to state my opinion. It was the first time in eighteen years as bishop that I criticized a government official. If you analyze the two declarations that I formulated, at no time did I speak about homosexuals nor did I make any derogatory reference toward them. In the first declaration I said that the judge's opinion was worrisome because it indicated a certain indifference toward the law, since a justice cannot alter the Civil Code in the first place, and she was altering it. At the same, I was alerting people to the fact that the head of the government, responsible for protecting the law, was prohibiting the appeal of this judgment. Macri told me that these were his convictions; I respected him for that, but the head of the Government does not have to transfer his personal convictions to law. In no moment did I speak disrespectfully about homosexuals, but, yes I did intervene and point out a legal issue.

SKORKA: In a democracy, everything should be resolved through legal channels by way of a sincere, respectful and extensive debate. Each side should argue in a way that seeks common ground with their adversary, in order to arrive at a successful judgment based on mutual concessions. There were those involved in the debate prior to the passing of the law who invoked "natural law," which presumes that nature itself contains rules that regulate human behavior; an undercurrent of this belief is the idea that G-d Himself incorporated this law into His Creation. But someone who is homosexual has every right to say that it was either G-d or nature that made him the way he is. There are those who add that homosexual love is deeper since they know about feminine and masculine love, even though that does not mean that it is the way families are created. Everyone knows the role that masculine and feminine figures play in the raising of a child and the problems that exist when these images are mixed up.

BERGOGLIO: It is often argued that a child would be better cared for by a same–sex couple rather than in an orphanage or an institution. Those two situations are not optimal. The problem is that the State does not do what it has to do. Just look at the cases of children who are in certain institutions, where the last thing that happens is recovery. There must be an NGO, churches, or other types of organizations that can take care of them. They should streamline the procedure of adoption, which are never-ending, so that these children can have a home. One failure of the State does not justify another failure of the State. The underlying issue must be addressed. More than a marriage law so that people of the same sex can adopt, we have to improve the adoption laws, which are excessively bureaucratic and, in their current implementation, encourage corruption.

SKORKA: It really is necessary to reform the adoption laws. The sages of the Talmud say that adopting a child is a supremely important act. Any legislation should take speed and efficiency into account after having analyzed the various stages of the adoption process. Returning to the topic of marriage, there is an element that we cannot leave out of the equation, as obvious as it is: love. There is a reason why the Bible uses the image of two lovers to represent the final stage in our search for G-d. As rational a man as Maimonides, a twelfth-century Aristotelian, defined the love between G-d and man in the same terms we use to describe the union of a man and a woman. Homosexuals love someone that they know, someone that is similar. It is easy to get to know a man, being a man. To get to know a woman is a much more difficult challenge for men—she must be deciphered. A man can understand perfectly well what another man is feeling just as a woman more easily understands what happens in the minds and bodies of other women. Conversely, discovering the "other" is a huge challenge.

BERGOGLIO: Part of the great adventure, as you said, is to mutually decipher ourselves. There was a priest who said that God made us man and woman so that we would love one another and be needed by one another. In preaching on marriage I usually say to the groom that he has to make the bride more of a woman and to the bride that she has to make the groom more of a man.

17. ON SCIENCE

SKORKA: Religion had served as a disseminator of culture in the broadest sense of the word until the Enlightenment. Whatever knowledge one had about any field of study was connected to religion in some way. That is why we find so many Jewish rabbis and Catholic monks who were dedicated to the various sciences. Maimonides, Copernicus and Mendel were some later examples of this ancient tradition. As an aside, scribes were typically monks as well. The Talmud is full of ideas related to sociology, anthropology and medicine. Religion was the channel through which culture and clarity of language were transmitted. It provided responses to the fundamental questions of life I mentioned earlier–What is Man? What is Nature? What is G-d? Even today, whenever important questions arise we still turn to religion–and these issues are tremendously important. For example, we had to re-define death in order to do organ transplants. Over the centuries, death was defined as the cessation of cardio-pulmonary activity. When the rabbis were asked if one could save a life by performing a heart transplant incorporating the removal of an organ that is still beating, they found that the concept of brain death already exists in the Talmud. One could say, "Look at what visionaries they were!"

Today we have arguments about when human life begins. Should we treat the inseminated ovum in its first stages of development as a person? According to the criteria of one of the Talmud's sages, it has already received a soul–the divine breath. Science has determined that a zygote already has all the necessary genetic information to develop into a new human being; but is that enough of an argument to conclude that it should be treated as a person?

When science reaches its limits, man turns to the spiritual–to the existential experiences of centuries past. Science and religion are fields that work in parallel and should be talking to each other. The scientist that tries to refute religious phenomena based on their studies is the same as a religious person who tries to refute science based on their faith–they are both foolish. Only through dialogue that starts by each recognizing their own limitations can debate develop between the two, which is absolutely necessary for humanity to move forward in its search for a base level of ethical conduct.

BERGOGLIO: It is true. On the one hand, as you said, Rabbi, there is everything that you mentioned about education, all the wisdom of the ages accumulated through reflection, by the Torah, by the Gospels, and it is offered to all of humanity. There is also another interesting thing: religious truth does not change, but it does develop and grow. It is like with the human being, we are the same as a baby and in old age, but in the middle there is a whole journey. In this way, as was explained before, something that was once seen as natural, is not seen like that today. One example is the death penalty: once it was one of the punishments that Christianity accepted, but today the moral conscience has become much more refined and the Catechism says that it is better that it does not happen.

Human conscience gets refined with respect to moral commands and it also grows in the understanding of the faith. The same happened with slavery: now it does not occur to anyone to put a bunch of people on a ship and send them to the other side of the ocean. It is true that today there are other types of slavery, like in the case of the people from the Dominican Republic who were brought here to be subjected to prostitution or the undocumented Bolivians who came to work here and were obligated to do so in inhumane conditions.

SKORKA: Often times, when religious institutions make mistakes, they own up to them, but sometimes they are silent or are reluctant to speak about them. To this day, the Church repents of the trial of Galileo. Just as a religious person who transforms their particular view of biblical texts into absolute scientific truth commits a sin of foolishness, so the scientist who believes that his knowledge is sacred and indisputable commits the sin of intellectual blindness. Science is constantly being updated, the constant challenge being to discover a theory that is better or more comprehensive than the existing one. As you said, Monsignor, there has been development in what we know about the spiritual, even though the essence of the spirit remains immutable. Without a doubt this process of development ought to include a dialogue between religion and science. It is not that one needs to make room for the other. However, when science cannot provide an answer, answers based on intuition arise that, for me, are then transformed into "spiritual" answers as they come from a spiritual process that is different from inductive or deductive reasoning.

Another thing to emphasize—and we must not forget this—is that science has its limits. Science does not seek to find out why things are—it only looks for the "how." The ultimate meaning of everything is something we do not know. To arrive at these answers we use our spiritual intuition. The "advantage" that science has with respect to religion is that one can go to the lab and prove the accuracy of the hypothesis, although there do exist some sciences, like psychology, where such a direct method of proof is not available.

BERGOGLIO: Science has its autonomy that must be respected and encouraged. There is no reason to meddle with scientists' autonomy, except when they overstep their field and get into the transcendent. Science is essentially instrumental in God's command when he says: "Be fertile and multiply; fill the earth and subdue it."[59] Within its autonomy, science transforms the uncultured into culture, but be careful; when the autonomy of science does not put limits on itself and goes forward. It can lose control of its own creation just like in the story of Frankenstein. It makes me remember a story that I read as a child in *El Tony*[60], that was called "The Mutants." Because of an overzealous science, people started to transform themselves into things. One clear example of these abuses is the possession of atomic power that can cause the destruction of humanity. When man becomes proud, he creates a monster that can get out of hand. It is important that science put a limit on itself and says: "Beyond this point, I am not creating culture, but another form of non-culture, that is destructive."

SKORKA: That's the moral of the story of the

---

59 Genesis 1:28
60 Ed. Note: *El Tony* is the most popular monthly comic book in Argentina.

Golem. In Prague, a rabbi created a doll, an automaton that could defend the Jews against anti-Semitic attacks. He engraved the word *emet*–Hebrew for truth–on its forehead, put the Tetragrammaton in its mouth and ordered the Golem to serve him. A version of this legend says that one Friday, prior to the arrival of the Sabbath,[61] the dummy was able to free itself and started destroying everything. The rabbi erased the first letter of the word on its forehead, which left it saying "*met*," which means death, and he took the little paper out of its mouth, at which point it turned back into the clay that the rabbi had used to make it. It is an archetype of what happens when man cannot control what he creates with his intellect–when the product of his creation gets out of hand.

---

61 Saturday, the sacred day for rest in the Jewish religion.

18. ON EDUCATION

SKORKA: Religion defines how we see our world and to educate means to pass on a worldview—that is why the two of them are so intimately connected. When we study how different cultures developed, we find two factors. The first is the society's technological progress. The other is the culture's development as evidenced by the values that inform the way its people live. Culture is essentially a response to three questions: "What is man?," "What is nature?" and "What is God?" Therefore, it is indispensable that in the course of their education, children study these questions along with the answers that religion has for them. Some might point out that in a democratic society they should be exposed to the full spectrum of ideas and not just one point of view. Of course I share that belief, which is why I am against having religious instruction in public schools as they have had in the past.

BERGOGLIO: I also do not agree with religion classes that entail discrimination against non-Catholics, but, yes, I do believe that religion must form a part of education in school, as one element in a wide open range that is provided in the classroom. It seems discriminatory to me that religion is not spoken of, that you cannot teach a religious point of view of life and historical events, as is done with other subjects.

SKORKA: I agree with you—we are taking a lot away from a child when we are denied the opportunity to teach them about religion. Now that being said, a more detailed religious education still needs to be provided by their parish or congregation. The basis of Judaism, which later became part of Christianity and Islam as well, is the exaltation of man as a being that is capable of behaving better by overcoming his natural instincts. The important thing that religion adds to education is the reaffirmation of man's sublime condition and how each person deals with it. The nation's public schools should provide some sort of religious education because their principal function is to transmit values. As soon as the concept of G-d is introduced, anthropocentrism gets nudged a little to the side. If they do not hear about G-d, children get the idea that reality centers on people, on themselves. Once the religious variable is introduced, one can then approach any of the other topics from a different angle. What is sex education? Is it only for answering questions about anatomy and physiology, or is it about basic values? Of course children need to learn about what is happening to them anatomically and physically but this has to be accompanied by specific values that will allow them to better decide what to do with their sexuality. Sex is supposed to be the way that man exhibits the strong emotions that come from being in love. At the time when a child is given that information, I would like it if the schools would say, "Judaism believes that . . ." followed likewise with the worldview of Christianity or Islam, accentuating the common denominators between them. If we were to abdicate our responsibilities to educate, we would lose our purpose. The only focus would be on how we are living today, in the here and now. With our religions, the concept of transcendence is essential–it means that what we're doing now does not just end with the acts themselves–they have an effect on the future. It is fundamental that we communicate this to the materialistic world we live in today.

BERGOGLIO: In the Bible, God shows Himself as an educator: "I carried you over my shoulders, I taught you how to walk," he says. The obligation of the believer is to raise their young. Each man and each woman has the right to educate their children in religious values. The effect of the State in taking away this right can lead to cases like Nazism, in which the children were indoctrinated with values different from those of their parents. Totalitarians tend to add water to their own mill.

SKORKA: We are always sending some kind of message to children, whether it is through what we say or do, or what we do not say or do not do. There is always a message. Why should we hand over that task to someone else? Religion is instruction to the man who is searching for the meaning of life. It is the same as when a philosopher discovers a truth that he wants to teach and share with others. He has to share the message with others—those that want to hear the message will and those who do not will not, but the information should be made available to everyone. It is something essential to every religion and there would be no religious institutions without it.

I want to make myself clear-speaking for Judaism (though I believe this is also true of Christianity)— religion is not just a question of worshipping and praying to G-d in a temple and that is that. In order to get to G-d, we can only do so through our fellow man. A religious person should express their feelings via a commitment to core values that reflect a belief in a life of transcendence. In my opinion, this information is what students should be taught so that it becomes a basic part of their education throughout their future course of study. As an aside—in the Jewish legal code, the laws that indicate how to honor one's ancestors can be found alongside those that reflect how we should honor teachers. One is integral to the other. Judaism is essentially an education—it is constantly teaching us something. Remember that the term *rabbi* means teacher.

BERGOGLIO: Schools educate toward the transcendent, just like religion. Not opening the doors to a religious worldview in the academic environment cripples the harmonious development of children because this concerns their identity, the transmission of the same values their parents have, which are projected onto the child. They are deprived of a cultural and religious inheritance. If in education you take away the tradition of the parents, only ideology remains. Life is seen with biased eyes, there is no unbiased hermeneutic even in education. The words are full of history, of experiences of life. When someone leaves a void, it is filled with different ideas from the family tradition; that is how ideologies are born. I remember that in high school there was a Communist professor. We had a wonderful relationship with him, he questioned us about everything and it was good for us, but he never lied to us. He always told us where he was coming from, what his hermeneutic and his worldview were.

SKORKA: We had a lot of teachers and professors in high school, but we rarely could talk to them about life. Some acted in such a way that they never left an opening to do so. But the kids asked themselves—this guy teaching me physics or chemistry—what does he think about how to make life better? Education cannot be something impersonal, there needs to be dialogue. The class became somewhat mechanical; they taught Euclidean geometry but nothing about the world's different points of view. There was no human touch, the lectures were sterile and had no message. There should be a consensus about respecting different points of view, but based on the transcendence of man, as understood in the broadest sense. Professors do not stray from the text very often—they do not open their heart. We do not want religion to restrict them, but we do not want them to be restricted from talking about it either.

BERGOGLIO: There is a difference between a professor and a teacher. The professor presents his material in a detached manner, while the teacher involves others; it is profoundly testimonial. There is also a coherence between his conduct and his life. He is not merely a transmitter of science, as is a professor. We need to help men and women to become teachers, so that they can be witnesses; that is essential in education.

19. ON POLITICS AND POWER

BERGOGLIO: The Catholic Church had a lot to do with the process of national independence in Argentina, a process that took place from 1810 to 1816. There were even priests in the First Junta, in the Tucumán Congress, in the Assembly of the Year XIII (October 1812). The Church was there at the hour that the homeland took shape, together with a mostly Catholic, evangelized and catechized people. When the homeland opened itself to immigration, communities with other beliefs began to arrive, like Jews and Muslims. Through this cultural and spiritual *mestization*[62] that

62 Ed. Note: The word *mestizaje* in Spanish means the blending of races and cultures that brings about a uniquely rich, varied cultural identity.

resulted, an Argentinean virtue was formed: here we live as brothers, despite the fact that there is always a crazy bomb thrower, some extremist. A symbol of this brotherhood is the city Oberá, the capital of *mestization*. There are seventy places of worship, of which only a few are Catholic; the others belong to other faiths: evangelicals, Orthodox, Jews, and all live together very well, very contently. Another example is that of William Morris, an Evangelical Protestant who left a mark on Argentinean education. The nation did not arise on the margin of religion, but in its light.

SKORKA: Without a doubt, religion, beginning with Catholicism, played a key role in the country's birth. The various religions that have found a home in Argentina have made important contributions to the national culture. There was a serious debate at the time of independence, when the clerics would hold discussions with followers of the Enlightenment–the other national independence movement that took their ideas from the French Revolution–to argue about what role religion should play in the affairs of the state. Now, I cannot say whether all those who said "no" to the Church were not really religious because it is easy to confuse the institution that guides the religion with the essence of the religion. The tension between the Enlightenment ideals of liberty, equality and brotherhood and religion turned out to be a very good thing since it forced both sides to analyze and revise their positions. As long as the debate was purely ideological, the result was positive. Looking at the situation in Argentina now: when a great crisis occurred–society looked to religion as its final refuge. When everything blew up in 2001, the *Mesa de Diálogo* was formed. Politics was broken and people called on religion to help find a way out of a difficult situation. Etymologically speaking, the word *iglesia* means "meeting" in Greek and *bet ha'knesset*, synagogue in Hebrew, means something similar–a "meeting house." What that means is that they are not merely places where one goes in search of G-d, but they are also where debates take place on every issue that affects people's lives. Just as it was in the past in the time of the Prophets, all religions need to clearly state their positions on social issues. Now, that does not mean that religious leaders have to play party politics. Monsignor, I do not know what you think about situations like that of Joaquín Piña,[63] one of your priests.

BERGOGLIO: Piña explained that it was not a political event, that it was about a referendum, but not about an elected office. He organized a voting process to see if there should or should not be constitutional reform. So, he resigned and left once he believed that he had fulfilled his duty.

---

63 Joaquín Piña is a Jesuit and bishop emeritus of Puerto Iguazú. In 2006, he led a civic electoral commission that managed to avoid the approval of an indefinite reelection project for the then-governor of the province of Misiones.

SKORKA: In my opinion, religion should stay on the sidelines with regards to politics, except in very specific situations, such as when Marshall Meyer got involved in defending human rights in Argentina. He always had very precise and well-defined goals—he did not want to be a congressman, senator or anything like that. He accompanied Raúl Alfonsín and other politicians on the path toward restoring democracy, but he never did it in the interest of obtaining a government post. We have to be extremely careful. We should never use the pulpit to further a political goal.

BERGOGLIO: We are all Political animals, with a capital *P*. We are all called to constructive political activity among our people. The preaching of human and religious values has a political consequence. Whether we like it or not, it is there. The challenge of preaching is to propose those values without interfering in that little thing called partisan politics. When I said, on the day of the anniversary of Cromañón,[64] that Buenos Aires was a vain, frivolous and corrupt city, someone demanded that I name names, but I was talking about the entire city. We all have the tendency to be corrupt. When a driver is stopped by a police officer for speed-

---

64 The Republic of Cromañón was a nightclub in the city of Buenos Aires and it caught on fire on December 30, 2004, while the band Callejeros was playing, causing the death of 193 people. That day, the capacity of the building was exceeded, the emergency exists were locked and the building didn't fulfill the insurance standards.

ing, often the first thing he hears is "how are we going to fix this?" We carry something inside that we have to fight against, that tendency toward using influence, toward the quick fix, toward that which would put yourself first on the list. We have the trait of bribery. In that homily I was talking about the defect of the city, I was not engaging in partisan politics. The problem of the press, truthfully, is that sometimes they reduce what one says to whatever is opportune. Today, from two or three facts, the media spins something different: they misinform. What is said from the pulpit refers to Politics with a capital *P*, to the Politics of values; but the press frequently takes it out of context and takes advantage of it for the benefit of lowercase politics. I remember that after the Te Deum Mass you said, "How courageous!" It seemed normal to me to speak like that, but you were already reading the interpretation that the media was going to give to my words. The next day, the daily newspaper gave my words various interpretations hostile to some politicians, but when I spoke of our leaders, I used the word "we" inclusively.

SKORKA: I remember that homily. It was on the May 25th holiday, and it was the one that resulted in the ban on Te Deum services at the Metropolitan Cathedral. Unfortunately, the media does not give the people a true sense of a religious leader's words, which are really just a call for us to maintain certain values. A religious leader does not just tell us how to look at specific current events, but instead tries to look toward the future, toward transcendence, appealing to deeply held values. From the very demanding point of view of the Prophets, if even one person goes hungry, things are not as they should be. Framed this way, what we have to do when we hear a homily is take a magnifying glass to it and pay attention to every word, studying it from the point of view of the Prophets. That all being said, given the importance of the Catholic Church in Argentina, it cannot avoid a dialogue with those in power, nor can it ignore the fact that the powerful will wind up interpreting its pronouncements politically.

BERGOGLIO: The risk that we must avoid is priests and bishops falling into clericalism, which is a distortion of religion. The Catholic Church is the entire People of God, including priests. When a priest preaches the Word of God, or when he reflects the feeling of the whole People of God, he is prophesying, exhorting, catechizing from the pulpit. Now, when a priest leads a diocese or a parish, he has to listen to his community, to make mature decisions and lead the community accordingly. In contrast, when the priest imposes himself, when in some way he says, "I am the boss here," he falls into clericalism. Unfortunately, we see in some priests ways of leading that do not correspond to the principles of seeking harmony in the name of God. There are priests with the tendency to clericalize with their public statements. The Church defends the autonomy of human events. A healthy autonomy is a healthy laity, where different competencies are respected. The Church does not tell doctors how to perform an operation. What is not good is militant laicism, that takes an anti-transcendental position or demands that religion not leave the sacristy. The Church gives values and the people do the rest.

SKORKA: As for me, I am very critical of, and skeptical toward the various political parties in Argentina. Unfortunately, recent history going back as far as I can remember has justified my feelings. I am not particularly faithful to any of the political parties. However, I always believed, and still believe, that the best social system is democracy. When I speak about Argentina from the pulpit, I speak generically—we are all to blame for what is going on. It cannot be that a country that can produce food for 300 million people is not capable of feeding all its 38 million inhabitants. That is a demonstration of how we have broken from our values. I constantly see people fighting for special interests instead of fighting for their neighbor's welfare. I also do not see any political institutions that hold deep convictions about changing the current situation. I warn people that politicians only fight to gain power and then use that power to put their interests before everyone else's. With very little money, we would have no more need for *villas miseria*.[65] It breaks my heart to see beggars in the street, a problem that seems to

65 Ed. Note: *Villas miseria*, literally "misery towns" is the Argentinean expression for shantytowns.

have increased tremendously. What we have is a sick Argentina. It pains my soul—our situation should be completely different. I am saying this without supporting any particular party and with the firm belief that at some point leaders will emerge that will be capable of changing the situation back to the way things used to be.

BERGOGLIO: A few years ago, the French Bishops wrote a pastoral letter whose title was "Rehabilitating Politics." They realized that they had to restore poitics because it was losing all credibility, and I believe that the same is true for us. The loss of credibility in the political arena must be reversed because politics is a very elevated form of social charity. Social love is expressed in political activity for the common good. I was born in 1936, I was ten years old during the emergence of Perón, but my mother's side of the family has roots in the radical party. My mother's father was a carpenter, and once a week a man with a beard would come and sell him aniline dyes. He stayed for a while chatting on the patio while my grandmother served them a cup of tea with wine. One day my grandmother asked me if I knew who Don Elpidio, the aniline salesman, was. It turns out that he was Elpidio González and had once been the vice president of the nation. That image stuck with me that this ex-vice president earned his living as a salesman. It is an image of honesty. Something has happened to our politics, it is out of ideas, out of proposals . . . They have shifted ideas of political platforms to aesthetic ideas. Today, image is more important than what is proposed. Plato said it in *The Republic*, rhetoric–which equates aesthetic–is to politics what cosmetics is to health. We have displaced the essential with the aesthetic; we have deified polling and marketing. Perhaps, that is why I am committing a sin against good citizenship: the last vote I cast was in the midterm election during the Frondizi Government.[66] I still have residence in the province of Santa Fe, because I worked there as a professor. When I came to Buenos Aires, I did not change my residency and since I was more than 300 miles away I was not going to vote. When I finally registered as living in Buenos Aires, I changed my residency, but I continued showing up on the Santa Fe voter registry. After all that, I turned seventy and I do not have the obligation to vote any more.[67] It is debatable if it is all right for me not to vote, but at the end of the day I am father of all and I cannot be wrapped in a political flag. I realize that it is difficult to disentangle myself from the electoral climate when elections approach, above all when some come to beat down the door of the Archdiocese to say that they are the best. As a priest, before an election, I send

66 Ed. Note: Arturo Frondizi was elected president of Argentina on May 1, 1958, and was overthrown by the military on March 29, 1962.
67 Ed. Note: In Argentina voting is compulsory, which makes not voting an act subject to fines. However, at the age of seventy, voting becomes discretionary.

the faithful to read the political platforms so that they can choose. In the pulpit I take care of myself rather well, I stick to asking people to look for the values and nothing else.

SKORKA: I also suggest that everyone read the party platforms and that they use their analytical skills to differentiate between them. I do not hold a position that is as politically exposed as yours, Monsignor, but when I am invited to a politician's event, as long as it does not have any connotation of electioneering, I go. I believe that it is a good way to honor both politics and the country.

BERGOGLIO: Of course, participating in political life is a way of honoring democracy.

SKORKA: On occasion, when certain politically charged events occur here at home, we issue some kind of opinion, and that opinion might be critical. When there is a position that is incompatible with our values, we should criticize it—but with religious arguments, not political ones. Since we are talking about social values, it is often difficult to separate one from the other—there is no way around it. On a TV show called *God Is My Rest*[68] I insisted on the importance of democracy during the military regime. It was not the type of criticism a politician would have made. Instead, it was that of a rabbi issuing it from his religious platform.

68 *Dios es mi descanso*

BERGOGLIO: There should be a distinction between politics with a capital *P* and politics with a lowercase *p*. Any act that a religious minister makes is a political act with a capital *P*, but there are some that would mix in politics with a lowercase *p*. The religious have the obligation to preach values, the lines of conduct, of education or to say a word, if requested, regarding a specific social situation. On December 30, 2009, I offered the Mass for the five–years anniversary of Cromañón. It was a social circumstance where I should say something. There are situations that call for that, when there is a serious deviation. It is not that one appears to the world through politics, but rather through the values that are at stake, through the tragedies that happen. The religious minister has the obligation to defend values; what happens is that the political world can become overly scrupulous: it listens to a pastor and they say that he is preaching against so and so. We do not preach against anyone; we refer to the value that is in danger and that must be safeguarded. The media, which are sometimes infected with hepatitis, and I say this because of their yellow color, jump out and say: "Harsh rebuke to so and so!"

SKORKA: Some politicians talk out of both sides of their mouths–on the one hand they ask that religious leaders do not give opinions, but during the campaign they want a religious minister's blessing.

BERGOGLIO: When I meet with politicians, some come with good intentions, and share a vision of the

Social Doctrine of the Church, but others arrive only to seek political ties. My response is always the same: Their second obligation is to have an inner dialogue between themselves. The first is to be a guardian of the sovereignty of the Nation, of the Homeland. The country is the geographical dimension and the Nation is the constitutional or legal aspect that makes social relations viable. A country or a nation can fall into war or be torn apart and be remade. On the other hand, the Homeland is the patrimony of the founding fathers; it is what we have received from those who founded it. It is the set of values that they handed down to our care, but not to guard them in a tin can, but to make them grow and launch them toward a utopia responding to today's challenges.

Once the Homeland is lost, it cannot be recovered; the Homeland is our patrimony. There are two images that tell me a lot about the Homeland. One is biblical: when Abraham leaves his land, following the path of God, and he takes his father who is an idol maker. Even then, he does not cut off his tradition but purifies it with Revelation. The other image is more Western: it is when after Troy is burned, Aeneas goes out to found Rome. The Homeland is carrying our fathers on our shoulders. With the inheritance that they have left us, we must negotiate the present, make it grow and send it forward to the future. Today the politicians are in charge of preserving the Homeland, the theocracies have never been good at it. God gives man the responsibility of managing the progress of his country, his homeland and his nation. Religion marks the ethical and moral guidelines and opens the path to the transcendent.

SKORKA: Monsignor, you used a key word—sincere and meaningful dialogue. Our country's worst problems are cultural more than anything else. Argentineans are not doing very well, and evidence of this is a lack of dialogue. Like you said, a country is a territory; a nation is a legal, judicial structure that provides order, and a homeland is the legacy of the past. All of these need to be fueled by values. Argentina, with its merits and mistakes, was created based on a framework where religion was an important factor. Even though each religious tradition has a different worldview, we need to bring them all to the table in a dialogue with agnostics so we can focus on the good ideas and arrive at a consensus as to how to restructure the homeland. I understand what you are saying, Monsignor, that we have to bring along our forefathers, but as the famous rabbi of Kotzk stated, when one truth tries to imitate another, it is not the truth anymore. Through dialogue, we have to create our own truth that has its roots in the past and which should include religion. That should be the point of contact with the world of politics. I should also mention that we are lucky that there are few theocratic states because that leads to fundamentalism. Every country should have a democratic system of government. I include the State of Israel where traditional Jewish values are evident in everything it does, via a system of government that is completely democratic. It is not easy, and there are constantly clashes between the State and religious authorities. The rabbinate will have one opinion and the Supreme Court another, and the country has to try and convince the religious authorities, who are sometimes very strict and unyielding, that democracy is the right way. Through dialogue, democracy softens hardened positions.

BERGOGLIO: Power is something that God gave to humanity. He told us: "Be fertile and multiply; fill the earth and subdue it."[69] It is a gift from God that allows people to participate in creation. I would question "power," which at times is used to define religion. If one thinks that power is to impose my way, to push everyone in my line and to make them go on that path, I believe that it is wrong. Religion must not be like that. Now, if I understand power in an anthropological way, as a service to the community, that is another thing. Religion has a patrimony and puts it at the service of the people, but if it starts to mix itself in superficial politics and to impose things under the table, then yes it can become a bad form of power. Religion has to have a healthy power, insofar as it serves the human dimen-

69 Genesis 1:28

sions for the encounter with God and the fulfillment of the person. There has to be a power that proposes: I help. It is not bad if religion dialogues with political power, the problem is when it associates itself with it to do business under the table. In Argentinean history, I believe there has been a little bit of everything.

SKORKA: Along those lines, in the Jewish community there is a before and after with regards to the AMIA (Asociación Mutual Israelita Argentina)[70] bombing. At the time, some in the community's leadership had become very close with the President of Argentina[71] but those relationships did not bear fruit. If anything, they bore bitter fruit. I believe that there needs to be dialogue, but at a distance. A friendship cannot exist if it is only based on the parties' taking advantage of one another. We have to be able to pick up the phone and call a cabinet member or the secretary of culture when there is a problem, but a clear line needs to be drawn. I know that in the Catholic Church, there were horrible priests like Christian von Wernich who were involved

70 Ed. Note: Founded in 1894, the Asociación Mutual Israelita Argentina (AMIA), located in Buenos Aires, is one of the oldest Jewish Community Centers in Latin America. On July 18, 1994, a car loaded with explosives smashed into the AMIA, killing eighty–five people, injuring over three hundred, and completely destroyed the building. Though the perpetrators remain unkown, the attempt has been connected to radical Islam. A new, modern eight-story building was inaugurated in May 1999.
71 He is referring to former President Carlos Menem.

in torture. Those like him were in a way supporting those procedures because they were giving absolution to the assassins instead of letting them know in no uncertain terms that they were assassins.

BERGOGLIO: Those that participate in situations like that are colluding.

SKORKA: A human being will never be anything other than a human being. We do not believe that men are angels, that are only capable of following orders and doing so with pure devotion. Whereas an angel does not have free will, man is influenced by his passions. At some level, the person who wants to lead a religious congregation has to have self-confidence, high self-esteem and at least a little bit of an ego. If they lack this, they cannot do it. Anyone that puts himself out as the head of a congregation needs to have his ego reaffirmed. There will always be questions like, "What is he going to do with that power?" because power is always used for something. Do you remember what I said when I called you about the election of the new Pope? "I hope that G-d enlightens the cardinals so that they can choose the right person." Historically, becoming Pope meant becoming an important voice, and even if it is always criticized, it is one that everyone cares about. I also hoped that they would choose someone with a mild temperament because that person might be called on to do very important things. The question is whether, when a person gets that much power, they can still be sincere and humble and if they are able to rise to the challenge. Fifty years ago this conversation would have been impossible and if it were not for you, it would still have been impossible. We have to break the vicious circles. As the head of the Argentinean Church, you used your power to do something. In contrast, we should not be constantly allowing mediocrities to get into positions of power.

BERGOGLIO: A very intelligent Jesuit told this joke: There was a person who came running asking for help. Who was pursuing him? Was it an assassin? A thief? No . . . a mediocre person with power. It is true, how sad for the people that are under a mediocre leader, who thinks too highly of himself. When a mediocre person thinks too highly of himself and gets just a little power, I am sorry for those that are under him. My father always said to me: "Greet people when you are going up because you are going to run into them when you come down. Do not think too highly of yourself."

Authority comes from above; now how it is used is another thing. It gives me goose bumps when I read the Book of Kings because there are only a few just men in the eyes of the Lord, but the vast majority are not. When one reads the things that our religious kings did, he feels like pulling his hair out. They even killed: the holy king, David, is not only an adulterer but also, to cover up what he did, he commands that the spouse of the woman be killed. But he has humility, when he is rebuked by the prophet Nathan, he recognizes that he has sinned and asks for forgiveness.

He moved aside and told the Lord to bring someone to replace him. Power is something that in our tradition is given by God: "You–says the Lord–did not choose me, I chose you." The day that I impose my hands on them and ordain them, I tell the priests that they did not study to graduate as priests, that it is not a career, they did not choose, but rather they were chosen. Now what happens? We are human, we are sinners, we are not angels, as you said, Rabbi. One can get entangled in powers that were not the ones given to him in ordination, but are of another kind. Or one can think too highly of himself, or impose a temporal power that is not the power that the Lord wants.

One good thing that happened to the Church was the loss of the Papal States, because it is clear that the only thing that the pope holds is a third of a square mile. But when the pope was a temporal and spiritual king, there was a mixing of the intrigue of the court and all of that. Do they not mix now? Yes, now they still do, because there are ambitions in the men of the Church; there is, sadly, the sin of careerism. We are humans and we tempt ourselves; we have to be very alert to take care of the anointing that we received because it is a gift from God. The circles of power, those that existed and exist in the Church, are a result of our human condition. But at some point, one stops being the one chosen to serve and becomes the one that chooses to live as he wishes, and his intentions are contaminated by his own flawed character.

20. ON COMMUNISM AND CAPITALISM

BERGOGLIO: In the immanent conception of the Communist system, everything that is transcendent and points to a hope in something beyond, paralyzes the work here. Therefore, as it paralyzes man, it is an opiate that makes him a conformist, it makes him bear his suffering, it does not allow him to progress, but this is not only the concept of the Communist system. The capitalist system also has its own spiritual perversion: to tame religion. It tames religion so that it does not bother Capitalism too much; it brings it down to worldly terms. It gives it a certain transcendence, but only a little bit. In both antagonistic systems, there is a vision of what opium is. The Communist system because it wants all work to be for the progress of man, a concept that came from Nietzsche. The capitalis system in turn tolerates a kind of tamed transcendence that manifests in a worldly spirit. For religious people, the act of adoring God means to submit to His will, to His justice, to His law, and to His prophetic inspiration. On the other hand, for the worldly who manipulate religion, it is not too hot or too cold. Something like: "Behave yourself, do some crooked things, but not too many." There would be good manners and bad customs: a civilization of consumerism, of hedonism, of political arrangements between the powers or political sectors, the reign of money. All are manifestations of worldliness.

SKORKA: Whether analyzing Marx' statement that religion is the opiate of the masses, or reading Nietzsche's assurances that man has killed G-d, I try to believe that these must be really intelligent people to ignore the importance of man's very real search for G-d. I try to make sense of their comments by looking at two perspectives. One relates to what you just said—Marx had no interest in G-d; he was interested in the here and now. He never wrote anything about expectations of spiritual transcendence. He thought that everything would fall into place if there were a more just socioeconomic order. Together with this, the other explanation would be that they were criticizing religious institutions which were lacking in spirituality. The Church, along with the other religions of that time, had failed to lift people up. There was a religious crisis at the time when Christianity was spreading throughout the world; people were searching for values to live by. If this were not the case, it would be hard to understand how such a great expansion could have happened so quickly. The religious Christian might say that Jesus' life was an event that had such an enormous impact that the whole world was moved and many accepted him immediately. Even given that point of view, from a historical perspective, there was fertile ground for change–pagan beliefs were in decline: creating a need for spirituality and Christianity was the answer to people's search. Something similar happened when Marx was alive, but the other way around. Religion did not have an answer for the spiritual yearnings of the time and that is why he wrote what he did. I think that perhaps all his rebelling came about precisely because he was searching for a great spiritual truth. In a similar vein, I feel that the modern world is becoming estranged from G-d as well and a lot of religious movements are joining in. They say, "If you just do this, everything will be alright. You will have a great afterlife." The religious experience is much deeper than that; it does not have the scientific certainty of a lab. It is a matter of faith that needs to be analyzed with extreme care and constantly revisited.

BERGOGLIO: Some people say that religion promises a better life if you put up with much more than human dignity should allow. The fact of a further reward does not exempt people from the obligation to fight for personal, social, ethical rights, for the Homeland, for humanity. If a person tolerates things without fighting for his rights, hoping for paradise, he is indeed under the effects of opium. The people that have suffered persecutions and destruction–like the three great genocides of the last century: the Armenians, the Jews, and the Ukrainians–fought, in a large part, for liberation. It might be that some have felt that they did not have enough strength and they entrusted themselves to God without having done what they should have. Catholic Doctrine says that human affairs have their own autonomy, that God gives it to them, and that one cannot exempt oneself from progressing by using paradise as an excuse. One has to fight for progress in every area: moral, scientific, educational and labor. We need to fight to keep from being drugged with opium.

SKORKA: Like the book of Psalms says, "The highest heavens belong to the Lord, but the Earth he has given to mankind."[72] We have to try to live balanced lives. When we lose that balance, we are lost.

BERGOGLIO: We inherited from Judaism the same concept. The Jewish people did not wait meekly for their liberation from Egypt. They allowed themselves to be led by the Lord with shrewdness and warfare. The Jews took possession of all of Transjordan by war, and when the Hellenists wanted to repress them, the Maccabees launched a guerilla war. They achieved their liberation doing what they had to do, and at the same time, they prayed. On one occasion, when they

72 Psalms 115:16

had everything prepared, they were afraid of the inferiority of their troops, and the prophet said to them: "Do not fear . . . for the battle is not yours but God's."[73] There were very few occasions when they were supposed to fight, and God exempted them. At times, God exempts someone from the effort to demonstrate His greatness. But the common thing is for Him to say: "I am with you, but you must fight." That was how Moses was, with both of his hands up, interceding while the people were fighting.

SKORKA: There is a teaching in the Talmud[74] that says that one hour of holding back and repenting, of returning to G-d and doing good deeds in this world, is better than an entire life in the world to come, and that one hour of tranquility of spirit in the world to come is better than a whole life in this world. To sum up, they are both extremely important. It is not right to make sacrifices during our earthly lives for the sake of the world to come. The same tractate of the Talmud[75] says, "The reward that the righteous receive for their labor will be given in a future life." It reminds me of, "Blessed are the poor in spirit, for theirs is the kingdom of heaven."[76] We should not necessarily take from this that we ought to live in a state of neglect and

73 2 Chronicles 20:15
74 Avot: 4:17
75 2:16
76 Matthew 5:3

poverty because that is the path to eternal life. I interpret the use of the word *poor* to mean that the accumulation of wealth is not necessary to obtain transcendence since doing good deeds alone is sufficient. According to the story of Genesis, G-d's mandate to man is to "have dominion over the Earth,"[77] which I interpret as living life here as fully as possible. Asceticism is not a Jewish ideal either, where one gives up even those worldly pleasures that are completely ethical while acting with honesty, justice and spirituality. In the Talmud[78] there is a statement that says that in the future, man will have to answer for all the beautiful fruit he saw but never tried. The Jewish ideal is not a world of submission and restrictions. As it says in Deuteronomy,[79] act with fairness and generosity so that you live life to the fullest both here and there.

77 See Genesis 1:28
78 Hierosolymitana, Kiddushin, Chapter 4, page 66, column 2, Halacha 12
79 6:18

21. ON GLOBALIZATION

BERGOGLIO: If we think of globalization as a uniform billiard ball, the richness of each culture is lost. The true globalization, that which we must defend, is like a polyhedron in which everyone is integrated but each player maintains his particularities, which, at the same time, enrich the others.

SKORKA: When I think of globalization, at first I tend to take a naïve view of things. For example, I think it is good that we can go to any airport in any country and not get lost since they all use the same symbols. In that sense, I think globalization is fantastic. But what I have a hard time understanding is how, all of a sudden, musical groups from the United States can become all the rage in Budapest. Due to these circumstances, movements have arisen that stress personal identity, which has also had an effect on Judaism,

Christianity and Islam. I do not think international deal-making between corporations is bad as long as there are rules and restrictions in place to ensure that society at large is not excluded from its benefits. Global interaction is good, but only if there are certain standards that prevent the destructiveness of materialism. I believe that there needs to be interaction among different peoples, as long as each group maintains their identity and strengthens it. An enlightened community knows to have enough confidence in itself to be able to look at what others are doing and decide what it likes and what it does not. It is what the Jews did after Alexander's invasion—the Talmud is full of Greek and Greco-Roman ideas since they could not just ignore the real achievements of those other groups. If people truly believe in themselves, they can have a meaningful exchange of ideas with others—that is how I see the globalization of cultures. However, when countries lack confidence in themselves, when they have no clear standards, when there is no consideration for one's fellow man, when men exploit other men, what you get is this uncontrolled flow of capital that we have been seeing recently.

BERGOGLIO: The globalization that makes everything uniform is essentially imperialist and instrumentally liberal, but it is not human. In the end it is a way to enslave the nations. As I said earlier, we must preserve the diversity in the harmonious unity of humanity. You mentioned some good things about the spirit of globalization that help us to understand each other better, but there can be other things that work against peoples. Here we often hear about the "melting pot" of races. If this is meant in a poetic sense, it is okay. But if it is meant in the sense of fusing nations, something is wrong: a nation has to maintain its identity and, at the same time, integrate itself harmoniously with others.

SKORKA: Those in Argentina who had spoken of a "melting pot" were hoping to create an Argentinean model by having everyone shed their skin and transforming themselves. They were extremists and were not looking for interaction to make us better.

BERGOGLIO: They were fundamentalists. A theme that characterizes Argentina's history is the mixing of races. That shows a certain universality and respect towards the identity of the other. I think that in Latin America–together with Uruguay, southern Brazil and part of Chile–is where the mestizo is most prevalent, in the good and rich sense of the word, where the encounter of cultures, and not their fusion, prevailed. I like it when all the different communities appear during festivities. For this reason I think the government was correct when, in their organization of the Bicentennial, they made room for all the communities, showing our diversity.

22. ON MONEY

BERGOGLIO: Christianity condemns both Communism and wild capitalism with the same vigor. Private property is real, but carries with it the obligation to put it at the service of others within just parameters. A clear example of what happens is the flight of money to foreign countries. Money also has a Homeland. Someone who operates a business in a country and then takes that money to keep it outside of the country is sinning because he is not honoring with that money the country to which he owes his wealth, or the people that worked to generate it.

SKORKA: The Bible contains an economic plan, which it lays out in the book of Leviticus.[80] What it says is that each person had their own plot of land. If

80 25

the owner could not work it, he could lease it, but the law tried to ensure that everyone had an inalienable claim to some property so that everyone would have the means to live with dignity. Undoubtedly, historical experience shows us that man needs to have an incentive to work. We have to look at why the Soviet Union failed, where there continued to be one class that maintained its hold on power and lived in luxury while a large part of the population lived in poverty. The abolition of private property was surely another of the key factors that led to its failure. The *kibbutzim*,[81] the twentieth-century experimental socialist agricultural settlements that were very successful, became one of the backbones of the State of Israel and made its creation and growth possible. However, they are no longer what drive the Israeli economy and they are looking at different methods of economic and social planning to survive. The idea of private property, fairly distributed with a fair redistribution of wealth, seems to be the right path. That takes us back to the laws and social order suggested in Leviticus. On the other hand, when the only things that are important to those who develop a society's social structure are the gods of money and consumerism and they fail to see mankind as the ultimate, essential beneficiary, the result is ruthless capitalism. As long as capital is used to help people, it is welcome, but if it is not, adjustments

81 Collective farms

need to be made with the goal of designing a more just social order.

BERGOGLIO: From this we understand the importance of the concept of social debt that we have among us. The dimension of social debt must be considered in every usufruct.

SKORKA: I teach my students that they do not need to show respect to those who are arrogant because they are wealthy and think they are in charge because they have money. Of course, when forming a congregation, in order to build it you need people of means, but the money must have been acquired honestly. It is not true that money has no name. You cannot build spirituality with blood money.

BERGOGLIO: There is a saying from a first century preacher that behind a great fortune there is always a crime. I do not think this is always true. I agree with what you say, Rabbi: some believe that by giving a donation they have cleaned their conscience. But, in a pastoral dialogue, the conscience is cleaned in another way. As I mentioned earlier, sometimes I ask the person that is confessing if he gives alms to the beggars. When they say yes, I continue by asking: "And do you look them in the eyes? Do you touch their hand?" And then they start to ramble, because many may throw a coin but turn their faces away. These are attitudes, gestures. Either you live in solidarity with your people or you live with your ill-gotten money. We have the seventh commandment: thou shalt not steal. Then there is the one who has ill-gotten money and wants to give it back with an act of charity. I never accept this kind of restitution if there is no change in conduct or verifiable repentance. Otherwise, the person washes their conscience, but the behavior continues. Once a religious director was accused of receiving money from a drug dealer and he said that he used the money to do good without asking where it came from. That is wrong. Blood money cannot be accepted. The relationship between religion and money has never been an easy one. People have always talked about the Vatican's gold, but that is in a museum. And also, we have to distinguish between a museum and religion. A religion needs money to manage its works; this is done through banks and is licit. What matters is the use one gives to the money received as alms or contributions. The Vatican's finances are public; it always runs a deficit. What comes in as donations or for visits to museums goes out to leper hospitals, to schools, and to African, Asian and Latin American communities.

SKORKA: It is impossible to create a perfect institution, even if it is a religious one, because man is imperfect. Every man is conflicted. Priests, pastors and rabbis are drawn to religious institutions for a variety of reasons. It could be for self-improvement or as a way to exercise self-control, but at some point they are going to derail. Not every clergyman behaves impeccably and that should not undermine the essence of religion. Just because one person slips up does not mean that one can infer that the whole thing is hypocritical. We have to separate the wheat from the chaff. What happens is that more is demanded of religion because it is based on morality. Anyone that talks about being faithful and then does things that are incompatible with moral values is doubly at fault, just like a judge who does not decide fairly, destroying his fellow citizens' belief in the justice system. During the dictatorship, those who were in charge of fighting the guerillas were doubly guilty because they went totally off the rails and ignored justice. The damage that they did to Argentina was horrendous, aside from that which they caused in the hearts of so many families. The same can be said of a politician who acts the wrong way—he is doubly guilty as well because he has an obligation to set an example.

BERGOGLIO: The worst thing that can happen to a religious person is living a double life, whether he is a rabbi, priest or pastor. In anyone else it could happen that they have their home here and their little love nest over there and it does not seem that condemnable. But for a religious person, it is absolutely condemnable. John Paul II was very blunt in this; in the mess left by the Banco Ambrosiano,[82] he ordered that they pay in full.

---

82 The Banco Ambrosiano was an Italian financial company that was founded in 1896 and that went bankrupt in 1982. In the middle of the collapse its president was Roberto Calvi, a member of the illegal Masonic lodge "Propaganda Dos" (better known as "P2"). The Vatican Bank was the Banco Ambrosiano's principal shareholder.

23. ON POVERTY

SKORKA: All religions have a complete and absolute obligation with regards to fighting poverty. Various parts of the Torah contain rules telling us that it is imperative to help the needy. The call of the prophets– especially the ones we call "Prophets of the Book"– Hosea, Amos, Micah and Isaiah–shows that one of the main points of their sermons was an absolute commitment to the poor. The way in which we honor G-d is by creating a just society, and that implies building a society where everyone can live with dignity. One of the basic theories that appears in sacred literature is that there cannot be a society, a town or a nation–and I would add a State–that lacks a strong ethical component and a commitment to people at every level of society. The obligation to help the widow and the orphan is repeated over and over again in biblical literature.

Jewish communities have a tradition of forming aid societies for those who need something to eat. In Argentina, the work of community assistance programs developed by the AMIA in conjunction with many other Jewish institutions is well-known. There has always been a commitment to help the needy. All the biblical writings regarding property rights try to guarantee that people do not accumulate vast estates–that each family has enough land to make a living and at the same time setting rules regarding the land that protect it from overuse. According to the Torah, every plot should be farmed for six years and it should rest during the seventh in order for nutrients to be restored to the soil. With regards to Argentina specifically, the country has always reacted to help the poor in times of crisis. Many sectors of our society have a deep-rooted custom of providing assistance to the poor. I remember when I was in elementary school there had been huge floods and I brought in blankets and boxes of clothes for the people who were affected by them. My family was very involved in helping out even though we were not very well-off. Our community has a history of providing assistance to both Jews and non-Jews. In my synagogue, Benei Tikva, we collect clothes to send to schools in Santiago del Estero and Pampa del Infierno in Chaco. It is heartbreaking to know that we are trying to help out while much of the rest of the country does nothing. It is not right that there are children who cannot go to school because they have no shoes to wear to get them there. We do not perform miracles; we are just trying to do what we can. After all, we are commanded to do so by the Bible, which says that a man cannot stand idly by while his brother suffers. I would also like to add something else—I would suggest that the Jewish people have been deeply committed to every struggle for human freedom and equality that the Western world has ever known. For example, during the Russian Revolution, the Jews had a huge interest in the outcome since it was all about an exploited class. They thought that through the revolution a solution would arrive for all of their suffering and hardship as Jews. We do not have to go that far back in history though. The percentage of Argentinean Jews that acted out of idealism during the social liberation movement of the seventies was much higher than the percentage of Jews in society as a whole. There were always Jews involved in the Communist and Socialist parties as well as all the other movements that sought to advance the demands of the lower classes. Even in the atheist Jew there remains the ancestral command to fight not only for one's own well-being. If another person is having a hard time, he also has to fight for him. Even if I am doing all right, it is not good enough if there are those who are not—we should all live with dignity.

BERGOGLIO: Christianity inherited the Jewish verse from Isaiah: Do not "[turn] your back on your own flesh."[83] The key is to be found in the parable of the Final Judgment, when the king places some people on his right and some on his left (the good and the evil, respectively). To those on his right he says: "Come, blessed of my Father, for I was hungry and you fed me; I was thirsty and you gave me drink; I was naked and you clothed me; I was sick and you visited me."[84] They ask Him when it was that they did this and He answers that every time they did so to the least of His kingdom, they did it to Him. The others, those who did not do so, are condemned.

In Christianity, the attitude we must have toward the poor is, in its essence, that of true commitment. And He added something else: this commitment must be person to person, in the flesh. It is not enough to mediate this commitment through institutions, which obviously help because they have a multiplying effect, but that is not enough. They do not excuse us from our obligation of establishing personal contact with the needy. The sick must be cared for, even when we find them repulsive and repugnant. Those in prison must be visited . . . It is terribly difficult for me to go to a prison because of the harshness of life there. But I go anyway, because the Lord wants me to be there in the flesh, alongside those in need, in poverty, in pain. The first attention we pay to poverty is assistance: "Are you

83 Isaiah 58:7
84 See Matthew 25:31–46

hungry? Here, here is something to eat." But our aid cannot end there. We must build toward human promotion and integration in the community. The poor must not be perpetually marginalized. We cannot accept the underlying idea that "We who are doing well give something to those who are doing badly, but they should stay that way, far away from us." That is not Christian. It's indispensable that we integrate them into our community as soon as possible, through education in technical schools . . . So that they may get ahead in life. This concept was dominant at the end of the nineteenth century in the schools created by Don Bosco for all of the destitute children he gathered into his oratory. Don Bosco thought that it made no sense to send them to public high school because it would not have helped them get ahead in life, so he created technical schools. Something similar is being done by the priests of the shantytowns of Buenos Aires. They seek to give kids, with a couple years of apprenticeship, the means they need to change their lives, to become electricians, cooks, tailors . . .

We have to help them earn a living. What is degrading to the poor is not giving them the oil that anoints them with dignity: a job. A poor man must not be looked at with disgust; he must be looked at in the eyes. Sometimes it may be uncomfortable but we have to be up to the task. The great danger—or great temptation—when aiding the poor, is falling into an attitude of protective paternalism that, at the end of the day, does not allow them to grow. A Christian's obligation is to integrate the most deprived into his community in whatever way possible, but definitely to integrate them.

SKORKA: After listening to what you have said, I would point out something else of interest–the idea of bringing people together is a reflection of the Torah's message. Everyone needs to be included. We have also created schools for the purpose of helping people out. Russia gave birth to the ORT schools, which at first also happened to be focused on the arts and trade. When they were founded they were meant for the poor, although now things have changed a bit. Although perhaps today it is more for the middle class and not a school for everyone, the underlying message remains that work brings dignity–it provides one with a profession so that he is able to face life's challenges.

BERGOGLIO: Christian charity is the love of God and neighbor. It can begin with aid, but it cannot stop at fundraising events. There are things that are called works of charity when, in reality, they are social-conscience calming activities. These kinds of programs are carried out in order to feel good about oneself, but love always requires a person to go out from himself, to truly give oneself to others. The person I intend to love needs me to put myself at their service. But there are many caricatures of charity. Have I told you the story about the gold Rolex?

SKORKA: No.

BERGOGLIO: Once, when I was bishop, I was sent

an invitation for a benefit dinner for Caritas. Those who attended were the cream of the crop, as they say. I decided not to go. That day, the president at the time was in attendance and, after the first course, a gold Rolex was auctioned off. What a disgrace; how humiliating. That was a bad use of charity. It sought a person who would use this watch for vanity in order to feed the poor. Thankfully, Caritas no longer does this sort of thing. Nowadays, they work continuously in schools, run shelters for single mothers and the homeless, run a bakery on the corner of Uruguay and Rivadavia Avenues, where they also sell the handicrafts that the kids in the technical school make. This is promotion of the poor by the poor themselves. Sometimes things are done in the name of charity that are not charitable; they are like crude caricatures of a good intention. There is no charity without love, and if vanity is part of helping the needy, there is no love; it is feigned charity.

SKORKA: I define charity as assistance that is urgently needed and extended to those in need quickly and immediately. In the biblical lexicon however, there is another concept that makes reference to helping the poor–*tzedakah*. The rabbis interpreted it as a tax that we should pay to help the needy. It is a word that has the same root as *tzedek*, which means "justice." This is where it seems that the idea arose that any society with people in need is intrinsically unjust and through *tzedakah* we can try to correct this failure, at least in part. Another concept that we find in Talmudic literature is that of *gemilut hasadim*, which can be translated as "acts of loving-kindness." It refers to the assistance one gives to his fellow man, whether by giving money or through action, whether rich or poor, living or dead; for the latter, making sure that they are properly buried. Every act of *tzedakah* should be performed with mercy. I believe that Christian charity combines both of these concepts in a similar way.

BERGOGLIO: The concept of *gemilut hasadim* made me think of the parable of the Good Samaritan, when Jesus asks who acted as a true neighbor and the people respond: "He who was merciful. He who took pity."[85] The second concept you mentioned, that which is linked with justice, was developed in Christianity in the Social Doctrine of the Church. It took quite some time to assimilate the concept of social justice, though now it is accepted everywhere. When someone takes up the manual of the Social Doctrine of the Church, they are astounded by the things it denounces. For example, the condemnation of economic liberalism. Everyone thinks that the Church is against Communism, and yet it is as against Communism as it is against the wild economic liberalism we see today. We have to seek equal opportunities and rights and strive for social benefits, dignified retirement, vacation time, rest, and freedom of unions. All of these things build social justice. No one should be dispossessed and there is no

85 See Luke 10:37

worse dispossession–and I want to emphasize this– than not being able to earn one's own bread, than being denied the dignity of work. There is an anecdote that may help us understand the Church's conscience on this issue: In the midst of one of the many persecutions in Rome, a deacon named Laurence was ordered by the emperor to hand over the treasures of the Church. On the designated day, Laurence went to the emperor, bringing with him a group of the poor. He said: "These are the treasures of the Church." This is the paradigm that we must protect because every time we leave it aside–either as a general institution or as a small community–we are denying our very essence. We glory in the weakness of our people, the ones we help to get ahead. The poor are the treasure of the Church and we must care for them. If we lose this vision of things, we will have a lukewarm, weak and mediocre Church. Our true power must be service. We cannot adore God if our spirit does not include the needy. I think we agree on this.

SKORKA: Absolutely. When a Jew arrived at the temple in Jerusalem with the first fruits, he went there to thank G-d for them. As it says in the Book of Deuteronomy in Chapter 26, at that moment one had to say, "My father was a wandering Aramean who had to go down to Egypt" because he was hungry.[86] These words make us think about poverty. Today, Jews and Chris-

86 Deuteronomy 26:5

tians share in the work of helping the poor. There is a tremendous spirit of cooperation between Father Pepe and Rabbi Avruj who work in the slums. Even though we rabbis have plenty of work to do in our own congregations, we dedicate part of our time to helping the needy who come knocking on our door. There are not that many of us, so we do not have a large organization that allows us to go and seek out those in need or have a larger presence in the slums and shantytowns. When a rabbi goes to a shantytown to provide assistance, it is not just to help Jewish people. We do not proselytize; it is a real commitment to help our fellow man. Since we are a small community, what we do not have are people that can commit themselves to go out to the slums on a regular basis to provide more in-depth support. Demographics have a large influence on what we can do. It is one thing for a priest to oversee the building of a new church where 90 percent of the people living in the neighborhood are Christian; it is another thing to build a Jewish temple since Jews do not have such a large presence.

BERGOGLIO: In historical terms, the shantytown priests are a relatively recent phenomenon in Argentina. It probably started some forty years ago and it took root with difficulty because it was new for the hierarchical structure of the Church. It was also the case that it had to be purified from political motivations because sometimes the religious and the political were improperly united, and that created mistrust. As long as the priests involved in this work were able to better define their belonging to the Church through popular piety, they brought about an attitude of greater closeness and comprehension in the hierarchy. At that time, in any case, the Archbishop of Buenos Aires was accused of preferential treatment toward the priests in the shantytowns. This is not a new phenomenon: in Italy, Don Bosco worked with the most humble and also provoked mistrust from the bishops. Not to mention, Don Cafasso and Don Orione. They were the avant-garde of work with the needy. In a way they forced a change in the authorities. Here, the shantytown priests have also caused a change in mentality and a change in the conduct of ecclesial communities.

24. ON THE HOLOCAUST

SKORKA: The Shoah[87] is an extremely important topic. There is the oft-asked question–"Where was G-d during the Holocaust?"–which we need to ask very carefully. That is because sometimes we like to say that we are beings with free will, but other times it is more convenient to question G-d as to where He was and why He did not do anything in the face of so much human brutality. Where was G-d during the Holocaust? I believe there are questions that do not have answers. There are things that we will never be able to understand, but it is clear that before we ask G-d where He was during the Holocaust, we should ask where the people were, both those who took action as well as

87 The Hebrew word for "devastation," used to refer to the Holocaust.

those who mercilessly and cruelly failed to act–those that murdered and those that looked the other way. The Shoah was not sparked by anger about a specific incident, but was a plot deeply rooted in European culture to exterminate an entire group of people simply because they were Jews.

BERGOGLIO: That question about God is not new. I remember one time–I must have been twelve or thirteen–we were going to a wedding with my family and the mother of one of the fiancés died a short time before from a heart attack, perhaps because of the excitement. We ran out of our house and went to the house of this woman and when we arrived, we passed by the son-in-law and he mumbled: "And they say that God exists." Christianity also lived through moments of adversity, of persecution. I agree that there are questions that do not have an answer. We always want to be content with an explanation, like children in the age of the "whys." Kids do not hear the answer and are already formulating a new question; what they want is for their parent to focus their gaze on them. With respect to the other question that you mentioned–Where was man?–that is the biggest contradiction to human solidarity of that period. The great powers washed their hands of it, they looked the other way, because they knew much more than what they were saying, just as they washed their hands of the genocide of the Armenians. At that time, the Ottoman Empire was still strong, and the world was in the midst of World War I and was looking the other way. The Shoah is genocide, like the others from the twentieth century, but it has a distinctive feature. I would not like to say that this is of primary relevance and the others secondary, but there is a distinctive feature, an idolatrous construction against the Jewish people. The pure race, the superior beings, they are idols for the foundation upon which Nazism was built. It is not only a geopolitical problem, there is also a cultural-religious issue. Each Jew that they killed was a slap in the face to the living God in the name of idols. A short time ago, I read—and it was difficult because it gave me nausea—a book with a foreword by Primo Levi that is called *Commandant of Auschwitz*, by Rudolf Höss, a coordinator of these extermination camps who wrote his memoirs while in prison. The coldness with which this man describes what happened there demonstrates the diabolical nature of the matter. The Devil presented himself in idols that tranquilized the human conscience.

SKORKA: You have touched on a sensitive topic—perhaps the most important one relating to the Shoah. Not too long ago the news appeared that a bishop in Krakow made a statement saying that the Jews had made the Shoah exclusively their own, downplaying the fact that other people were harmed as well. There are people that argue that the Jews and their six million murdered are just a small part of the fifty million victims of World War II. However, the point is that the Jews did not die fighting for a political cause and they were not part of an army. Regardless, neither of these reasons would have made it justifiable and it would have been just as abominable. What the Shoah was about was exterminating a people merely because they belonged to a particular group that shared the same culture and faith. Maybe the murderers believed they were challenging the God of Israel. Maybe that is why the massacre was called a Holocaust (from *holo* meaning "sacrifice" and *causto*, which means "fire" or a sacrifice thrown onto a fire). Whoever came up with that name probably considered the crime a sacrificing of the Jewish people to the pagan deities created by the Nazis. In Hebrew, it is called the Shoah, a biblical term that means "devastation," to make sure that we're clear about what happened. It was a devastation of human beings executed by other human beings. In Poland, there were an incredible number of war victims, but they were not like those of the Shoah. That is because the Poles, Latvians, Lithuanians and Ukrainians were present at the concentration camps and showed the worst of themselves by joining in on the destruction and devastation of the Jewish people. The Nazis tried to erase the concept of Judeo-Christianity from the world. One of Marc Chagall's pieces shows Jesus being crucified while wearing a tallis.[88] There is also a menorah burning at his feet and scenes of violence all around him–synagogues set ablaze, elderly

88 A ritual prayer mantle of the Jewish people.

Jews fleeing the scene, trying to save the sacred scrolls of the Torah; frightened women and children running away. I have always said that in the death camps, they did not just kill six million Jews, but they killed Jesus six million times over. That is because many of Jesus' ideas and his message were Jewish since he carried the message of the Prophets.

BERGOGLIO: This is a very Christian belief: Jesus is in every suffering person. We complete in our suffering what is lacking in Christ's Passion.

SKORKA: It is also found in Talmudic thought. When we study the death penalty in the tractate of Sanhedrin, it says that even when a transgressor is punished with the death penalty, G-d suffers along with him.[89] Even at the moment that the punishment is meted out, G-d is with him. I agree with you wholeheartedly.

BERGOGLIO: In the book that I just mentioned, I discovered terrible things. They removed teeth from the Jews, they cut their hair and went to the extreme of choosing other Jews to take over these tasks. They led them to apostasy; it was a way to transfer the blame to them. One satanic detail: it was no longer the Nazis' fault, but rather the Jews themselves. The subtlety and the hate that is behind all of this is stunning.

SKORKA: Monsignor, what do you think about how the Church acted at the time?

89 Mishna Sanhedrin 6:5

BERGOGLIO: A few years ago, Cardinal Clemens August Von Galen was beatified because he confronted the Nazis. I do not know how he saved his own life; he was a very courageous bishop who from the beginning denounced how Nazism operated. Pius XI spoke perfect German and in that language wrote an encyclical that, if one reviews it today, has not lost its topicality. It is the one that starts, "It is with deep anxiety . . ." Initially there might have been bishops who were a little bit more naïve, who did not believe that the situation was so grave. The same thing happened in our country, some went to complain immediately, others took longer, it was not so clear. When the Vatican realized it, they started to give passports to the Jews. When Pius XII died, Golda Meir sent a letter acknowledging that he had saved many Jews. The Nunciature in Italy operates from a house in Rome, with a park that is a donation from a wealthy Jew in gratitude for the action of the Church on his behalf. Some survivors went later to thank the Pope. The Vatican has houses that are extraterritorial, in Italy, in which they hid many Jews. I am speaking about the positive side. On the other hand, I heard that the Church did not say all that it should have said. Some believe that, if it were to have done so, the reaction would have been much worse and it would have been unable to save anyone. In order to shelter some Jews–they say–the statements were more cautious. Who knows if we could have done something more. Recently, serious historians, a Jesuit among them, published exhaustive studies vindicating the action of the Church.

SKORKA: That's the question Monsignor. Could it have done more? I have an interesting anecdote to share regarding Von Galen, the German bishop from Munster. Fritz Steinthal, the rabbi that founded my congregation, was a German who survived Kristallnacht, which that took place in the early morning hours of November 9–10, 1938, when the Nazis destroyed most of the country's Jewish synagogues and businesses. In his memoirs, the rabbi noted his appreciation for Von Galen and other Christian priests who saved Jews while putting their own lives at risk. Now, with respect to the actions of Pope Pius XII during the Shoah, it is very difficult to form a conclusive opinion because people have written both for and against him. Just as we have Golda Meir's letter that you mentioned, there are books that claim that he did not speak out as much as he could have. The World Jewish Congress is asking the Vatican to open its archives. I think that it would benefit everyone involved if we investigate what happened down to the smallest detail and review everything over and over again until we find out where the mistakes were made. It is the only way to make sure it does not happen again. I believe that self-criticism, when it is warranted, is the only way to move forward. I do not know enough about the theological reasons behind the analysis supporting the beatification of

Pius XII and I do not question that he had been a very important leader of the Church. The great existential doubt that I have is how could he have kept quiet when he came to learn about the Shoah? What kept him from shouting about it in anger from the rooftops? Prophets cry out against the smallest injustice. What would have happened if he had cried out? Would consciences have been awakened? Would more German soldiers have rebelled? I am not saying that these things would have happened, I am just trying to put myself in the place of those who suffered, those that do not have a voice anymore, as if I were talking to them and sharing their pain. Should some be saved if it means others will be abandoned? According to Jewish law, when an enemy army surrounds a city and declares that they will murder everyone in the town if an innocent person is not handed over to them to be killed, the whole town should let themselves be killed. No one has the right to choose who is saved and who is not.

BERGOGLIO: What you said about opening the archives relating to the Shoah seems perfect to me. They should open them and clarify everything. Then it can be seen if they could have done something, to what extent it could have been done, and if we were wrong in something we will be able to say: "We were wrong in this." We do not have to be afraid of that. The objective has to be the truth. When one starts to hide the truth, one eliminates the Bible. One believes in

God, but only to a point. One is not being fair. We must not forget, we are sinners and unable to stop sinning, even though it is also true that God does not want it like that; He loves us with His mercy, but if I do not recognize that I am a sinner, His mercy does not get to me, it does not reach me. We must know the truth and go to those archives.

SKORKA: Another controversial topic in Jewish-Vatican relations was Benedict XVI's decision to allow certain congregations to pray once again for the conversion of the Jews.

BERGOGLIO: The original prayer, in Spanish, was strong: "We pray for the perfidious Jews . . ." Even though in Latin, the adjective means "those that do not have faith," John XXIII erased it with a stroke of a pen.

SKORKA: John XXIII was the one who paved the way for a worldwide dialogue. It began when he was the nuncio in Turkey where he saved a lot of Jews by giving them fake baptismal certificates. When he assumed the papacy, he pushed for significant change. In him, we could really see what it means to be a pastor. John XXIII was someone who took action, worked things out, spoke out and took risks. The big question is whether Pius XII really risked at all, not only with regards to the Jews but to the whole world. I would go even one step further—I ask myself if he risked as much as he could have for the Church. There are certain times in life when you have to take specific action, because if not, then when are you going to do it? These are the questions that eat away at me.

BERGOGLIO: I heard many times that John XXIII granted false birth certificates to Jews, but I have not confirmed it for myself.

SKORKA: Actually, the Raoul Wallenberg Foundation has all the documentation proving it is true. One of the organization's missions is to make the public aware of the heroic actions of ambassadors and other important people who put their lives at risk on behalf of the Jews. Perhaps, to get a better understanding of some of what happened, we have to look at each of the Popes' backgrounds and the kinds of education they had. Pius XII was educated in the environs of the Vatican and his family was connected to the Holy See. He was part of a group that believed that anything could be achieved through diplomacy, and that if a solution could not be found through diplomacy, then there was no solution. Roncalli, John XXIII, came from a humble family and a small village where people were taught how important it was for everyone to take care of one another through quick, practical solutions–the complete opposite of diplomacy. Therein perhaps lies the reason for the differences between the two popes.

BERGOGLIO: I insist, we would have to read what the archives say. If there was a mistaken vision or something else. I do not have concrete details. So far, things that I have seen seem to strongly favor Pius XII, but I also recognize that not all the archives have been reviewed. Besides, you are right: John XXIII, until the moment of his death, continued being a rural peasant. On his death bed, his sister placed on his head cold cloths with vinegar, just like they did in the country.

SKORKA: Pius XII was not very interested in Judeo-Christian dialogue. He was actually averse to it. After World War II, there were members of the Church who worked hard to change that attitude. The change did not begin until John XXIII became Pope. When he received a delegation from the World Jewish Congress, they say that he extended his arms and said, "I am your brother Joseph." That is the phrase that Joseph used when he made peace with his brothers. Obviously, things had not always been that way. For various reasons there had been a certain animosity present. There are books that have documented the anti-Semitic feelings that have existed within the different Christian denominations over the course of the last twenty centuries. There have been priests who have preached against us, while there have been others who maintained a real and very respectful dialogue. There have also been moments in history where people brandishing crucifixes incited the local population to commit pogroms and other acts of outrageous violence. There were magazines in Argentina in the 1920s and 1930s that declared themselves Catholic that preached hatred of the Jews.

As for today, I believe that the point of this dialogue we are having is to break these vicious cycles; to get a fresh start and to remind us of our shared heritage. If some people believe that Jesus is G-d made flesh, and we say that G-d would not do that because no human can represent G-d in bodily form, that discrepancy is no reason to breed hate or resentment. Some day we will know the truth, but in the meantime we can and we should be working together. Our ethical foundations have many commonalities that unite us.

One can easily correlate what the Gospels say to the positions of the Talmudic sages. Much of historic anti-Semitism had to do with the instigation of hate for opportunistic or political reasons. For example, in Russia when Tsar Alexander II was killed, the Jews were blamed, and then the churches were used for political reasons to get the masses riled up. There is no question about this, it is a proven fact. The question now is, "How do we start over?" If the two religions want the same thing, a world at peace, each one has to take the best of their traditions and row in sync with the other. We can help build each other up. The inaugural lecture given by Abraham Yehuda Heschel at the Union Theological Seminary, a Protestant institution in New York, was called "No Religion Is an Island." We cannot be broken apart and separated as we were before World War II. Our messages have to be generic and for everyone's benefit; not to pursue a change in each other's identities but to draw us near and bring us closer to each other.

BERGOGLIO: There is a phrase from the Second Vatican Council that is essential: it says that God showed Himself to all men and rescues, first of all, the Chosen People. Since God is faithful to His promises, He did not reject them. The Church officially recognizes that the People of Israel continue to be the Chosen People. Nowhere does it say: "You lost the game, now it is our turn." It is a recognition of the People of Israel. That, I think, is the most courageous thing from Vatican II on the subject. Moreover, the Jewish People can no longer be accused of having killed God, as they were for a long time. When one reads the account of the Passion it is clear. It would be like if all the Argentinean people were blamed for a specific governmental administration.

SKORKA: In reality, the government of that time was not even in the hands of the Jews. Pontius Pilate and the Romans were the ones making the political decisions. On top of the cross on which Jesus was crucified, they put the acronym INRI,[90] meaning "King of the Jews." If he were indeed King of the Jews, that would mean that He was undermining the foundation of Roman authority. Besides, crucifixion was not a penalty that the Jews applied when someone was condemned to death. Moreover, at that time, the Sanhe-

90 Iesus Nazarenus Rex Iudaeroum

drin[91] had already stopped handing out death sentenc-
es. And even if the opposite were true, they would not
have been able to carry it out on Passover. And even if
some well-known Jews had said at the time that Jesus
was not the son of G-d, what right does anyone have,
so many generations later, to blame their descendants?

BERGOGLIO: Indeed, you cannot speak about a
people that killed God, but I do not want to pass over
something we started to talk about. You said that in
Argentina there was also—and there is—ecclesiastic
anti-Semitism. I did not have the experience of John
Paul II, who at school, had Jews as half of his class-
mates, but I have and have had Jewish friends. Maybe
one of them was called "the Russian," as we used to
call [Jews] when we were children. I never had any
problems with any of them. There are, as there were,
anti-Semitic Catholics, but not with the virulence of
the '30s, when there were some churchmen who took
that line. Today the policy of the Argentinean Church
is clear: interreligious dialogue. One has to say that the
pioneers in this direction were Cardinals Jorge Mejía
and Antonio Quarracino.

SKORKA: Mejía did a lot of work with Marshall
Meyer. Together they founded the Instituto Superior

---

91 That was the name in ancient Israel for an assembly of
wise men composed of twenty–three judges in each Jewish
city. The Great Sanhedrin was a supreme court with seventy–
one members of the people of Israel.

de Estudios Religiosos.[92] Also, where Quarracino is buried there is a display containing fragments of Hebrew prayer books saved from the different concentration camps along with other documents relating to the Shoah. He wanted it to be there, in the Metropolitan Cathedral.

BERGOGLIO: There was some pressure from certain groups to remove those things and transfer them to the Cathedral's museum, but I did not approve it and nothing came of it.

92 The Instituto Superior de Estudios Religiosos (ISER) is an organization that brings together Catholics, Protestants and Jews. It was founded in 1967 to promote mutual harmony and understanding, but also to analyze national reality from a theological perspective. The institute included personalities such as the Catholic theologian Jorge Mejia, who, thirty years later, would become a cardinal. The great promoter of ISER in the beginning was Rabbi Marshall Meyer.

25. ON THE 1970S

SKORKA: The conduct of the political hierarchy of the Jewish community, and specifically that of the DAIA (Delegación de Asociaciones Israelitas Argentinas), is often questioned regarding what they did during the era of the National Reorganization Process.[93] However, during that same decade, the Conservative Movement began to have greater influence and its leader Marshall Meyer did publicly defend the disappeared.[94]

93 Ed. Note: The Proceso de Reorganización Nacional or "National Reorganization Process" was the name used by the leaders for the military dictatorship that ruled Argentina from 1976 to 1983.

94 Ed. Note: *Desaparecidos*, "disappeared," became a noun used to refer to people arrested and never seen again during the military government in Argentina that ruled the country from 1976 to 1983.

He himself said that it was a lonely struggle, but he did as much as he could to get involved. That is why when Raúl Alfonsín was later elected president, he recognized Meyer's work by inviting him to become a part of the Conadep.[95] Marshall told us that after listening to hour after hour of testimony, he was sickened by what he had heard regarding the horrors that were committed. I remember that I went with him and a group of his students once to sign a petition requesting that they free Jacobo Timerman,[96] but the DAIA was against it and in the end it was never published. It is very hard to pass judgment on the leadership of the community. As you said, Monsignor, every action needs to be judged and analyzed based on what life was like at that time, given the specific situation, circumstances and dilemmas. It is not easy to accuse someone of lacking bravery, honor or serious commitment. But when someone occupies an important position in the community and he remains in that position even though he does not speak up after events like those that occurred when the military ran the government, he deserves to be looked

95 The national commission for disappeared persons, Conadep was an organization created by Raúl Alfonsín to investigate the human rights violations during the previous military dictatorship. The final report was published under the name "Never Again."
96 Director of the daily *La Opinión*, who was kidnapped by the military dictatorship and later expelled from the country.

at with a critical eye. There comes a time when one has to decide to play along or resign. They even kidnapped the son of Nehemias Resnizky, who was president of the DAIA at that time, and there were rumors that he made a deal with the military authorities in exchange for his son's release. Whoever investigates this topic has to come to understand and unravel the problems of the time to find out what the DAIA really did and did not do. I do not like to judge people prematurely, but what I can say is that there were others who acted differently when they found out what was going on.

Marshall Meyer had a totally different attitude. His actions had a great impact–he was not an Argentinean citizen, but an American–yet he brought the call of the prophets into our midst. We still have the speeches and sermons that he gave, calling for human rights in Argentina–at the time, they were truly eye-opening. Marshall Meyer opened doors for everyone; what he did at the time–what we did in following his example–was to help prevent further injustice. Those of us who were close to him during those awful years got involved in some way, to a lesser or a greater extent. For example, he designated Felipe Yafe, one of his students, to help form the Cordoba chapter of the Conadep. I myself had a television program–*God Is My Rest*–toward the end of the dictatorship where I spoke about the importance of democracy and other issues that were not in line with the military regime's ideas. There are those that defend the DAIA's leadership during that time, but there are also inescapable truths—on one hand there are the enormous number of the victims' family members who criticize the DAIA and on the other Meyer proved everything that could be done and that the authorities did not do. His positive results prove the failure of the community's leadership.

BERGOGLIO: In the case of the Catholic Church it is more complicated because of the historic relationship that was maintained with the State. The Church always preferred from the beginning to lobby rather than make public declarations, although there were some, and right after the coup. In the book[97] that was edited to mark the twenty-fifth anniversary of the document "Church and National Community," in the third chapter it speaks about human rights,[98] and it mentions the declarations from May 1976. There were bishops who realized immediately what had happened; the case in point was that of Bishop Zazpe, who learned that the mayor of Santa Fe was savagely tortured and responded swiftly. Others who also realized immediately and fought were very worthy men like Hesayne, Jorge Novak, Jaime de Nevares. There were also Meth-

97 *Church and Democracy in Argentina*, Conferencia Episcopal Argentina, Buenos Aires, 2006
98 Pages 625–728

odists, like Aldo Etchegoyen. They were people who worked in every way for human rights, who spoke, but also acted. There were others who did a lot, who did not speak much, but saved people; they went to the barracks and fought with the commanders.

At that time, I was thirty–nine years old and I had been the Jesuit Provincial since 1973. I had a very limited view of what was happening because it is very different from being a bishop with a jurisdiction. I was moving on March 24, 1976, without knowing what was going to happen that day, even if it was foreseen; the curia was at 300 Bogotá Street and we had decided the previous year to move to Máximo College in San Miguel. By chance we picked that date; therefore, while we were moving the furniture, the country was trying to understand what was happening. The police even came in the middle of the move and asked us what was happening. In that place, San Miguel, a lot of people received help. We organized spiritual exercises and had available to us the theology and philosophy departments with more than two hundred rooms. We hid several people for days. Later, some came out on their own and others waited until someone could take them out of the country or they found safer hiding places. That is when I realized what was happening. What did the Church do during those years? It did what any organization does that has both saints and sinners. There were also men that are a mix of both of those characteristics. Some Catholics made mistakes, others moved ahead correctly. There were Catholics who justified their actions with the argument that they were fighting against Communism. One thing that disoriented and scared many was how the guerrillas in Tucumán had been positioned, which is what led President Isabel Perón to sign the famous decree that ordered the destruction of the guerrillas. The terrorist attacks also scared many. I remember the painful massacre of the recruits in Formosa. The horrors committed during the military government were discovered only little by little; for me it is one of the biggest scourges that hangs over our Homeland, but that does not justify the bitterness, the hate that does not fix anything. We cannot be naïve either; that many people who lost their children would have these feelings is understandable, because they lost flesh from their flesh and they do not have anywhere to go to cry for them. Even today they do not know what happened to them, how many times they were tortured, how they killed them. When somebody criticizes one of the Madres de Plaza de Mayo groups, the first thing I do is ask that they put themselves in those mother's shoes. They deserve to be respected, understood, because all of that was terrible.

Summarizing a bit: in the Church there were Christians from different groups, Christians killed as guerrillas, Christians who helped save people and repressive Christians who believed that they were saving the Homeland. There were different types of clergy; the Episcopal Conference lobbied, and many times. It also made public statements. I agree with you that we have to do significant investigation. But it cannot be assumed that there was a simplistic complicity.

SKORKA: I think that the question that one has to ask oneself is what power did the country's social leadership really have at that time? In the DAIA's case, they had the moral authority that came from being the representatives of the Jewish people on a national level. What power did they really have? There were some specific cases where I tried to find out what had happened to a particular person and all the doors I knocked on were closed to me. I was very young and I did not have any connections at the time. But I still have to ask–those that were our leaders and held positions of authority–did they have the instincts necessary to do the right thing? I am not just talking about the Church, but about all those who had some influence or power in Argentina at that time. Did they have it and were afraid of losing it? Why did they not shake things up? I think about all of Argentinean society– all those that could have knocked on doors and could tell the military that to fight the guerrillas they should just bring them to trial. Under no circumstances should they have made people "disappear." That was horrendous.

BERGOGLIO: During the military government of

Augusto Pinochet, the Chilean Church acted along the lines that you mention, and created the Vicariate of Solidarity. It took a decisive path. As I said before, there were statements and quiet lobbying here, and that gave rise to all kinds of speculation. I, for example, in the book *El Jesuita,* had to clarify the accusations that were made against me regarding the case of two priests.

26. ON SOME HISTORICAL FACTS: THE CONQUEST, SOCIALISM, AND PERONISM

BERGOGLIO: When we speak about the participation of the Church in the Spanish Conquest, we have to realize that the American continent was not a harmonic unity of native peoples, but rather the strongest empire ruled over the weakest, and they already lived in a state of war. This was a reality, there were peoples subjugated by the strongest, by the most advanced, for example, by the Incas. The historic interpretation has to be understood from the hermeneutic of that time; as long as we use extrapolated hermeneutics, we distort history and become unable to understand it. If we do not study cultural contexts, we make outdated interpretations that are out of place; just like what happens when we talk about the Crusades. Nowadays we do not understand the reasoning behind the Crusades, but there was a time when each side killed each other; the Turks were kicked out of the Holy Land of Jerusalem ... When Catholics sacked and destroyed Constantinople, what theological explanation can you give? It is a major sin, but, culturally, in that period, they did things like that. That indicates the brutality that we sometimes have inside. At that time, there was a concept of bringing the faith, that was linked to the sin of the conqueror: the faith was imposed even by cutting off heads. We cannot analyze history from an ethical, purist point of view. History has always been like that, regrettably, with or without faith. This has to humble us. In that period, faith and sword went hand in hand. A historical analysis always has to be performed with its own hermeneutics from the period, not to justify the events, but rather to understand them. It is essential to analyze history in the cultural context of the moment in which the events occurred. Thinking according to how we live today, for example, Abraham's sacrifice of his son, Isaac, would be incomprehensible. We have to study history according to the conceptions and practices of that period. Another important issue is to analyze historical processes in their entirety and not remain with a fragmented interpretation, because that fragment then becomes universalized, and takes the place of the entirety and it becomes a legend. Just as it has been pointed out how bad the Spanish were–evidently they came to conduct business in these lands, and to take away the gold–during the period of the Conquest there were men who were dedicated to preaching, to helping, like friar Bartolomé de las Casas, defender of the natives abused by the conquerors. Almost all of them were meek men and they became close to the natives and treated them with dignity. They had to have come into contact with different customs, like polygamy, human sacrifice, and alcoholism. In the missions, the Jesuits invented *mate* to help the natives pass from their addictions—to alcohol, to *chicha*[99]—over to something that was not harmful but that would also give them some energy. There was a great advocacy effort that many men in the Church supported that did not want to entangle itself with the exploitative civil authorities. Roque González, for example, was a Jesuit saint; he fought with his brother, who was something like the governor of the city of Asunción, because he disagreed with the enslavement of the natives. The Church defended the natives; the Jesuit missionaries are an example of human advocacy.

SKORKA: Regarding the era of the Spanish Conquest, there was no Jewish participation to speak of. The only thing that one could point to is the arrival of the crypto-Jews to the Rio de la Plata. We should not forget that it has been documented that in 1810 a petition arrived from the Inquisition Tribunal of Lima asking for the extradition of someone who was ac-

---

99 Ed. Note: *Chicha* is a native alcoholic drink made out of fermented corn.

cused of being a crypto-Jew. All of this was researched by Boleslao Levin. However, there really was not any Jewish influence on a socio-political level until a large number of Jewish immigrants began to arrive in 1880 when the agricultural colonies in the interior of the country–Moisesville and Mauricio, among so many others–were formed with the help of Baron Hirsch, which helped to fulfill the dream of Juan Bautista Alberdi, who wrote in his book, *Las Bases*, that one of the keys to Argentina's growth would consist of attracting European immigration. Jewish participation in Argentinean culture first appeared in the sciences and in literature as represented by Alberto Gerchunoff, Bernardo Verbitsky and Cesar Tiempo as well as by important doctors. Political participation did not begin until the second wave of immigration in the 1910s and '20s, when people came from Turkey and Eastern Europe who brought their socialist ideas with them. That is why we see a Jewish presence in politics, particularly in the workers' movements, in the Socialist Party–such as the well-known Dickman brothers–and in the Communist Party. There were also anarchists like the famous Simon Radowitzky, who assassinated Chief of Police Ramon Falcon. Later on, the Jewish community became deeply involved in the fight against Nazism. Here I am talking about Jewish culture, because as you know, Judaism is a global outlook, a group of values, but not all of its adherents necessarily comply strictly with the rules of the religion. Back then, the engine of Jewish culture was based on the ideals that the immigrants brought over from Europe where they were organized into political groups, which they then brought over here. Also at that time—we are talking about the '20s and '30s—there was a very important stream of Zionism that longed to bring its socialist ideology to the land of the Patriarchs. On the other hand there was another group, the Bundists, who were also socialists but thought that the Jewish community should participate in global affairs. In either case, it explains why the Jewish community participated in Argentinean politics with a socialist ideology. With regards to the Jewish view of Perón, speaking of something that deserved and continues to deserve a lot of scrutiny, what we can say for certain is that he let Nazi scientists and assassins into the country, while on the other hand he recognized the State of Israel at the beginning of 1949 and had a good relationship with the Jewish community. There was a rabbi—Amram Blum, who officiated at the Gran Templo on Calle Paso—who had close ties to Perón. For its part, the DAIA wanted to maintain its distance from the government. It was the only time that the community was divided in two as exemplified by the formation of the Organizacion Israelita Argentina, which aligned itself with Peronism. Those years, the 1930s and '40s, were not easy times for the Jews. There were groups in the Church that came out against our community and made some very harsh pronouncements. There were very nationalistic and anti-Semitic groups–it was nothing at all like it is today.

BERGOGLIO: It was a period of peak nationalism that was somehow unjustly fused with Catholicism. Even today there are magazines that publish the ultranationalists and in them they accuse me of having fallen into heresy because I dialogue with other sectors, but I want to highlight the social dimension that the European Jews brought with an anecdote: One day an elderly man came up to see me. He presented himself and told me that he had come to speak on behalf of the retirees. It was Don Julio Liberman, the former director of the Guild of Tailors during the Perón period. He was a Communist, an Argentinean, and a son of Polish parents. As a child he had returned to Poland, but he came back here to enlist and stayed. We started to talk and I found him very friendly and–over all–with a great attitude; every now and then we would chat. One time he told me that he was going to be honest with me, he was not a believer. He belonged to that group of socialist Jews that you mentioned. He was ninety–two years old. He was a tough Jew, of the kind that when he left his union, because of his age, he continued to fight on behalf of the retirees. The social struggle that brought over those European Jews did a lot of good, it stirred the social conscience of Argentina. I suspect that the majority were not believers, like Julio told me.

SKORKA: No, he was not a believer. However, if we are honest and think about it, we know that it is extremely difficult to arrive at an exact definition and dividing point as to where faith ends and ideology begins. Some might say that all those Jews were socialists because they came from humble homes; they felt in their bones the pain of poverty and social injustice. But there were others who also lived under those same conditions and nevertheless did not wind up becoming socialist ideologues. At the same time, I wonder about those people who struggled with G-d and what weight the socialist ideas of the Bible had on them, given such forceful declarations by the prophets, especially Amos, Jeremiah and Isaiah, who relayed very clear messages in G-d's name, calling on the conscience of the people to ensure social justice. This then gives rise to another doubt. Perhaps they were not fighting with G-d; maybe they were fighting against the religious structures.

BERGOGLIO: That's how it was, in the case of socialists from Catholic tradition who strayed away from religion and fought for the social cause; they generally had conflicts with the religious structure, with ways of living religiously where some believers–instead of being a bridge–become a wall. They become an impediment to their own faith because they use it for their own advantage, for their own ideology or merely to accommodate themselves. We can mention, as a defect, some worldly arrangements made by certain sectors of the Church with power. Another defect is in charity work, in the sense that little Susan, from Mafalda,[100] would practice it: "I do a fundraiser with tea, with many sandwiches, teacakes and other delicacies to be able to buy polenta, noodles, and that rubbish that the poor people eat." That charity is neither Christian nor social, and it does not come from faith. It comes from what you said, Rabbi: if a priest today were to preach as Amos, translated into Porteño[101] so that he could be understood, they would try him as a Communist, as radical, and they would all but try to throw him in prison. The Word of God is much stronger regarding social justice than what we ourselves can do or say, or what our own communities would be willing to tolerate. It is impressive. During the '70s there was a little bit of everything, but social engagement flourished. At that time, a priest could not engage in a style of charity like little Susan, but rather he had to be shoulder to shoulder with the needy. What happened is that in some cases they fell into the trap of becoming ideological. There were priests who later left the ministry and

100 Ed. Note: "Little Susan" or Susanita is the most unsympathetic and judgmental character from *Mafalda*, one of the most popular comic strips in Argentina. Similar to Charlie Brown, most of the characters that surround Mafalda, who is the melancholic, though philosophical, protagonist, are children.
101 Ed. Note: "Porteño" refers to slang used by people from the harbor on the Rio de la Plata and by extension to all of Buenos Aires, which lies on the river.

remained estranged from the Church's healthy development and suffered repression at the hands of the establishment. In those years, there were rebellions from priests in Rosario, in Mendoza, where the discipline, the religious and the social, were all mixed up. Another thing is the harshness of the prophets. During the first centuries of Christianity, there are many examples, like the homilies of Saint John Chrysostom. If today a priest were to recite those, they would scandalize half of the congregation, because—just like the prophets did—he called things by their name. The Church has always had a social commitment. It is enough to see that religious congregations in Argentina had orphanages, schools, and hospitals. There were men and women that were dedicated to the social issues. The priests that went to work with the marginalized are not a novelty from the '70s; already in the 1970s there were sixty–eight nuns who were assisting the sick and died during the yellow fever epidemic. Later, the laity started to take charge of social welfare with the appearance of social welfare societies. The Fundación Eva Perón deserves special mention. When Evita proposed a path of social commitment that would start in the Secretariate of Labor, and later in her foundation, there arose a conflict with the Beneficent Society because she moved things further, she brought in more social integration. Look, Rabbi, in the beginning the Church did not confront Perón, who was close to certain members of the clergy; Perón wanted to use elements from the

Social Doctrine of the Church and incorporate many of them in his books and proposals. One of the men that provided him with these elements was the bishop of Resistencia, Bishop De Carlo. He was a good friend of the Peróns and helped them write some of their social books. He collaborated a lot with them, to the point that the Peronist Government constructed a seminary for him at the roundabout near the entrance to the city of Resistencia. Every time that Perón went there, he spoke from the balcony of the seminary to the people gathered at the roundabout. De Carlo was looked down on, and was accused of being too involved in the new politics. He was a great pastor, he said that he never compromised his conscience, and it is true.

There is an interesting anecdote: During one of those visits to Resistencia, Perón said to the people that were listening that he wanted to clarify one calumny: "They say that Bishop De Carlo is a Peronist. It is not true, Perón is a Decarlist." Initially there were some Christians who helped Perón explain his social path. Now, together with that sector coexisted another, more liberal one, that gathered together the anti-Peronist current. These were the ones who joined the Radical Civic Union, who, with the Conservative Party and with the socialist core, created the Democratic Union at election time. Initially, the Church remained associated with the Perón regime, and even obtained things such as religious education; whether that was good or bad is something else. After Evita died, the distancing began. Perhaps the hierarchy did not know how to handle the circumstances well and the conflict ended with the '54 showdown. When I was a boy I remember reading an article in the daily newspaper: "The gentlemen and monsignors of the bountiful table." That was the first attack. The mutual confrontation continued from thereon out, and many innocent lives were taken. The nationalist group within the armed forces did not care about the civilian inhabitants of Plaza de Mayo, and they sent their planes, which had the incredible inscription "Christ Conquers." That disgusts me, it makes me very angry; I am outraged because it uses the name of Christ for a purely political act. It mixed religion, politics and pure nationalism. Innocent people were killed in cold blood. I do not accept the argument that it was done in the defense of the Nation, because you cannot defend the people by killing the people. It is simplistic to say that the Church only supported or only opposed Perón. The relationship was much more complex, it came and went: first there was support, later some leaders were in bed with them, and finally there was a confrontation. Rather complex, like Peronism itself.

I would also like to clarify that usually in journalism when they say "The Church" they refer to the bishops, the priests, the hierarchy; but the Church is the entire People of God. In those days, those who would later be called "little black heads" continued being Catholics and fervent Peronists, despite the fact that the government was trying to burn the churches.

27. ON THE ARAB-ISRAELI CONFLICT
AND OTHER CONFLICTS

SKORKA: When people talk about the Arab-Israeli conflict, they generally do so based on the latest images they have seen, while completely ignoring the history behind them. I believe it is essential that the escalation of violence be put to a stop immediately. As Anwar Sadat[102] said when he visited Israel: "We will have plenty of discussions, but there will not be any more wars." Weapons need to be silenced—we have to find a way to live together in peace and keep working at it. Unfortunately though, there are interests that benefit from the current situation, even as Israelis cry for their victims and so very many Palestinian people live in the Gaza

102 Anwar Sadat was the president of Egypt from 1970 to 1981. In 1978, he signed the peace agreement with Israel known as The Camp David Accords.

Strip in terrible, wretched conditions. Besides those that try to take advantage of the conflict, we have the international markets, with their cold-hearted calculations that value barrels of oil over human life. In addition, the fundamentalists also find it useful since they feed off of, and are sustained by, conflict. Iran needs this conflict to exercise its influence in Syria and Lebanon through Hezbollah, and in Gaza through Hamas. They dream of rebuilding the "Great Persian Empire," restoring the Shiites to power and subjugating all those that do not agree with theocratic rule by the ayatollahs. There was a time when a huge peace movement grew in Israel. In Hebrew, it was called "Shalom Achshav" or Peace Now. Unfortunately, there was no similar organization on the other side. At no time did I ever see a gathering of two hundred thousand Palestinians shouting "Let's make peace!" When Barak[103] met with Arafat[104]–and this is documented–he granted everything that the Palestinian leader demanded, including a part of Jerusalem, which was very risky for Barak because it is the feeling of right-wing Israelis and many Jews generally that Jerusalem is eternal and indivisible. Arabs pray facing Mecca and we pray facing Jerusalem. In the name of peace, however, part

103 Ehud Barak was the tenth prime minister of Israel from 1999 to 2001.
104 Yasser Arafat was the leader of the Palestinian Liberation Organization and later president of the National Palestinian Authority.

of Jerusalem would have been administered by some type of Palestinian government. Nevertheless, Arafat kept asking for more, and it all fell apart. Barak returned to Israel and had to resign because he failed to reach a peace agreement. Arafat, on the other hand, went home and was greeted as a hero. Of course there has to be a Palestinian state–there are people who identify with the Palestinian nation. Whenever this does happen, it means that Israel will have found a genuine partner to negotiate with–should G-d wish it to be a democracy. The most prized and quintessential desire of the Jewish people is peace. The ending of Chapter 19 of the book of the prophet Isaiah is very powerful. It talks about a time when there will be an agreement between Egypt, Israel and Assyria–perhaps we should take that to mean Syria–and that this pact will be a blessing for the entire world. We have to change the terms of the discussion; we have to change what I call "disgraceful politics" into a desire for greatness. Religious themes are often invoked in a twisted form and in the most harmful way. There have already been so many people killed, and atrocities committed, in the name of G-d, something that we have mentioned in many of our previous talks. As you said, people were killed here in 1955 in the Plaza de Mayo in the name of Christ. Today, in the Middle East, people are constantly killing each other in G-d's name. This situation can only be turned around if both parties have a desire to rise above themselves–when people no longer want to take the crusts of stale bread away from their neighbors and others no longer want to destroy their neighbors because they live better. Why not transform the Gaza Strip into the Hong Kong of the Middle East? Why not convert it into a place where its people can really live very well? What matters is the life of each individual and that a Jew has as much right to live as a Palestinian; but the Palestinian also has to understand that. I am not talking about the men in the street, but their leaders; the ones who think that by destroying others they are doing a great deed by which they will be remembered for eternity. All types of extremism are bad and any group of people that thinks it should rule the world is evil. Sometimes I think about why G-d had to make the world round, and the answer I come up with is that every point on the globe is equivalent. There is no point more important than the other—they are all the same.

BERGOGLIO: You moved from giving a political explanation about a particular juncture to a discourse full of wisdom about human relationships. I recall a conversation that I had a long time ago with an older person who was going through an intense spiritual moment, and reviewing his life in a certain way, he told me that he had a family problem that he had not been able to resolve. "It is one of the failures of my life maybe because I never found the way," he told me. That phrase has stuck with me. Sometimes, human relationships can be resolved if there are people who help find the way, because when one has a problem only a mountain can be seen ahead and nothing else. Somebody has to say, "It would be better if you go over here, or try over there." When I have a problem with someone, it helps me to have the same attitude that the Egyptian monks had at the beginning of Christianity. They accused themselves so they could find a solution; they put themselves in the defendant's seat to see what things were not working well inside of themselves. I do it to observe how things are not working well inside of me. This attitude gives me the freedom to, later, be able to forgive the fault of the other person. The mistake of the other person does not need to be emphasized too much because I have my own mistakes and both of us have failures. The harmony between people is made by searching for ways; that is what I thought that you were underlining behind your reflection, Rabbi. That is the manner to resolve animosities.

SKORKA: Culturally, we are living at a time when the media has a huge impact. It infuriates me that they argue about every topic as if it were a soccer match. Things are not so black and white—they are much more complicated—but they deal in fanaticism and make false and superficial arguments. The only thing they aspire to do is focus on the latest headlines and create sensations. On the other hand, most thought-provoking books that deal with political or social issues are written using highly technical language or in philosophical terms that are over people's heads.

Then there are a lot of very capable people who use their shrewdness to argue their positions with lots of passion, but the truth can only be attained through humility and they lack the necessary restraint. The media has gotten accustomed to presenting the Israeli-Palestinian conflict this way.

BERGOGLIO: The media's way of putting things, in black and white, is a sinful tendency that always favors conflict over unity. You spoke of humility, which is what levels the paths for an encounter; favoring conflict only puts obstacles in the path, and the Spirit of God manifests itself in that leveling. Georg Händel beautifully took up that issue in the beginning of The Messiah, in the baritone's voice with the text from Isaiah: "Every valley shall be lifted up, every mountain and hill made low," so that the path shall be flat, to prepare the path to salvation.[105] To search for ways is a prophecy toward unity. What you said about the media, I would extend to all those that highlight conflict, to those that speak in black and white. Today, there is misinformation because only part of the truth is said, only what interests them is taken for their convenience, and that does a lot of damage because it is a way of favoring conflict. If I read five newspapers, comparing the same story, it is very often that each one will emphasize the part it is are most interested in according to its inclination.

105 Isaiah 40:4

SKORKA: I have been thinking about the issue of conflict . . . When I read Freud, what I like about what he says is that man needs to resolve his conflicts and that the way in which he does so then determines what he will actually do. A doctor could not practice his profession if he did not have some level of aggression, because to take up a scalpel—or perform the simple acts of giving an injection or taking blood—is somewhat violent by nature. What happens is that the doctor channels it into something positive. It is important to study what each person does with their aggression and destructive tendencies. I believe—and this is not Freud's invention but something that already appeared in the rabbinical texts more than two thousand years ago—that we have good inclinations and evil inclinations, and the idea is to know how to take these evil inclinations and try to transform them into something positive. When conflicts are not resolved with this in mind, we get the world we are living in today, because the aspect of humility is lacking. Moses got to be the most important prophet for various reasons, but principally it was because he was the most humble of men.

BERGOGLIO: Conflict is present in the first few pages of the Bible. We have the case of Adam and Eve who are expelled from the Garden of Eden, and there is also the drama between Cain and Abel and later the conflict of the Tower of Babel or the conflict of Rebecca with Esau and Jacob. During Jesus' life, his disciples created tension all the time. This means that in religious life conflict is to be anticipated. Even more so, we could not understand Revelation, the Bible, if we did not seriously consider conflict. The issue is how conflict can be resolved according to the Word of God. I believe that war must never be the path to resolution, because that would imply that one of the two poles of tension absorbed the other. Neither does it resolve in a synthesis, which is a mix of the two extremes–a hybrid that has no future. The two poles of tension are resolved at a higher level, looking toward the horizon, not in a synthesis, but in a new unity, in a new pole that maintains the virtues of both, it assumes them, and like that it can make progress. It is not an absorption, nor a hybrid synthesis, it is a new unity. If we look at genetic codes, this is the manner in which humanity advances. A true philosophy of conflict would have the boldness and courage to seek to solve both the personal conflict as well the social, seeking a unity that reunites the virtues of both parts. There is a quote from a German Lutheran theologian, Oscar Cullman, that refers to how to bring together the different Christian denominations. He says we should not seek that everyone, from the outset, affirm the same thing, but instead he proposes that we walk together in a reconciled diversity; he resolves the religious conflict of the many Christian denominations by walking together, by doing things together, by praying together. He asks that we not throw rocks at each other, but rather that we continue walking together. It is the way of advancing the resolution of a conflict with the virtues of all, without nullifying the diverse traditions or falling into syncretism. Each one, from their identity, in reconciliation, seeking the unity of truth.

SKORKA: Man lives in conflict, wherein lies his greatness, and his possible downfall. There is a place in the Talmud that says that man has both angelic and animalistic traits. The angels are completely spiritual beings but they do not have free will as they simply comply with G-d's commands. Man, on the other hand, does have free will, animal traits and spiritual traits. These characteristics are in constant conflict with each other.

28. ON INTERRELIGIOUS DIALOGUE

SKORKA: A priest once pointed out to me in Mar del Plata that there were religions that had not been participating in our national celebrations, and although it is a tradition, it could still be changed. That stuck in my mind.

BERGOGLIO: I do not know if you remember, when I began the Te Deum Masses as Archbishop, I came down with the nuncio accompanying the president and we walked him to the door. All of you, representatives from other faiths, would remain in your place, like puppets in an exhibition. I changed that tradition: now the president goes up and greets all of the representatives of the other faiths. That was a step in the direction that you propose. Since the Te Deum in Salta in 2009, the ceremony is divided in two: not only is the traditional, classic, song performed, and the Eucharist, together with the homily and the Catholic prayer, but the representatives of other faiths also present their own prayers. Now there is greater participation.

SKORKA: For me, these gestures mean a lot; it is a way of showing the importance of interfaith dialogue.

BERGOGLIO: Your work in this area is very important; I did not forget how you invited me twice to pray and to speak in the synagogue, and I invited you to speak to my seminarians about values.

SKORKA: Your attitude has also been important and courageous since there must have been people within the institution that did not think the same way.

BERGOGLIO: The first time that the Evangelicals invited me to one of their meetings at Luna Park, the stadium was full. That day a Catholic priest and an Evangelical pastor spoke. They gave two talks each, interspersed, with a break to eat some sandwiches at noon. At one point the Evangelical pastor asked that everyone pray for me and for my ministry. He had asked me if I would accept that they would pray for me and I answered him that of course I would. When they prayed, the first thing that occurred to me was to kneel down, a very Catholic gesture, to receive their prayer and the blessing of the seven thousand people that were there. The next week, a magazine headline stated: "Buenos Aires, *sede vacante*. The Archbishop commits the sin of apostasy." For them, praying together with others was apostasy. Even with an agnostic, with his doubt, we can look up together to find transcendence; each one praying according to his tradition. What's the problem?

SKORKA: There is a book that was written by a very dear friend, a very special rabbi named Shmuel Avidor HaCohen. He was much older than I and was among the founding members of the Israeli pacifist movement Peace Now. He was a revolutionary in many respects. Shmuel wrote the biography of another legendary rabbi, Abraham Isaac HaCohen Kook, who in the first half of the twentieth century, said that all those who designed and built the *kibbutzim*, despite their estrangement from tradition, performed a religious act because they returned to the Land of Israel when it was still occupied by the Turks and it was all swampland. For him, it was a religious act to recover the dignity that comes through working the land, something which had been denied to the Jews of Europe. That was like your kneeling at the Evangelical service–he was a man rowing against the current. That is why Shmuel called his book *Man Against the Current.* From that point of view, I appreciate the changes that you introduced at the Te Deum–that the president greets all of the religious dignitaries, and that some of them also give sermons. Changing those things within such an ancient organization is not easy. I congratulate you for trying to break old, vicious cycles. That is our work, and our challenge.

29. ON THE FUTURE OF RELIGION

SKORKA: Religion will always have a future because it is an expression of the profound search for the meaning of life and a consequence of introspection and encounters with Him. As long as life continues to be a mystery and man wonders who created the natural order—while those questions, which I believe will be eternal, persist—the concept of religion will endure, as a manifestation of the urgent calling to understand who we are. As long as he does not have answers to these questions, man will desire to become closer to G-d, and that in essence, is mysticism. Now, as to what religion will look like in the future, that is another story. I have absolutely no doubt that man will retain his religious sensibilities. What we do not know is how they will be organized and what form they will take.

The big questions are whether the religious institutions that we are currently familiar with will continue to exist and whether traditional religions will continue to develop. That is where other variables come into play.

BERGOGLIO: Saint Augustine has a quote that goes in the direction of what you were saying, Rabbi. He says: "Lord, you have made us for yourself and our hearts are restless until they rest in you." The most important part of this prayer is the word *restless*. If we are being honest with ourselves there is a feeling of profound restlessness behind our search for the transcendent, one that stirs us to an encounter with Him. As we live the encounter, another search is initiated and so on and so forth, each time with more depth. We like to describe that restlessness like the breath of God that we carry inside of us, the mark that He left in us. Many times it is even in people who have not heard God speak or who have taken anti-religious stances in their life, or were immanentists, and all of a sudden, they encounter something that transcends them. While this restlessness continues to exist, religion will continue to exist, there shall be ways to be bond with God. The word *religion* precisely means to come to assume a bond with the Lord by means of searching. If a religion is purely ritualistic, without this type of content, it is destined to die because it fills you with rites but it leaves the heart empty. I agree with you that religion will endure, because restlessness is inherent in human nature and we will have to see what it will be like in the future. How do you see it?

SKORKA: It is very difficult to know how history will unfold. As we can see from biblical accounts, religion essentially begins with individuals–Abraham, Moses, the Prophets–they approached G-d, who then told them to return to the people because that closeness to G-d needed to be revealed to the community. That initial seed, that personal dialogue, begins to weave itself into the fabric of daily life, along with other ideas and other motivating factors. The result is a very beneficial exchange, because a religion that cannot be expressed as part of one's daily life will never rise to be more than a mere philosophical game. The Jewish belief is that religion is how we live our lives. As the Torah says, "Do what is right and good in G-d's sight." However, when we work toward making the spiritual practical and we lower it to the level of our daily routines, different motivating factors start to come into play and they become interwoven with our religious experiences. Many times, those factors overpower the purity and beauty of the encounter, and they end up distorting it. That is why to talk about the future of religion means talking about the future of mankind and of history; it is almost like making a political and sociological projection. I have heard some Christians mention a return to a type of parochialism, which is an idea I am in favor of. Instead of there being hierarchical mega-institutions, the idea is to return to smaller congregations that nurture their own spirituality. It would mean having more independent bodies. I do not know if you have heard any talk of this idea; I like the idea of not working with huge groups of people, but instead with groups of very active families that interact in coordination with other groups of the same faith to work on large-scale projects—like social services, for example—while still maintaining their independence. Another thing I have heard is that in Europe there are people who have begun to search for their identity back before the pre-Phoenician era, which is very interesting to me because it is a deep search for their roots, and not a forward-looking vision. How will this influence the religious attitude of Europeans? Within Judaism, what we are seeing in Latin America is a revitalization of the extremes, both on the right and the left. The middle path has been lost. How is our present situation going to change over time? The truth is that I do not know. To me it is always interesting to see what is happening with our neighbors in the Christian Church, because there are trends that tend to appear in all religions at the same time. And when I look at what is happening across the street, I find that there is a very great crisis, where new churches are emerging that are perhaps looking to detach themselves from a central authority that does not satisfy them. After the French Revolution, the fragmentation of society returned in the form of nationalism. Since then, there have been various attempts to re-create the great empires of old, but sooner or later they collapsed and fell apart like Yugoslavia, which continues to break itself up into smaller pieces. I understand the parochialism that I am talking about to mean that everyone goes back to their roots. Now, we cannot know if this new situation will allow us to achieve peace, or at least lead to a state of not being at war. There is no way to know if selfish or hidden motives are going to prevail. What the prophets tell us—and of this I am sure—is that if we can get to a situation where dialogue predominates over small-minded interests, religion will flower, regardless of the level of parochialism.

BERGOGLIO: If one looks at history, the religious forms of Catholicism have varied notably. Let us think, for example, of the Papal States, where temporal power was united with spiritual power. It was a deformation of Christianity, it did not correspond to what Jesus wanted and what God wants. If, throughout history, religion evolved so much, why wouldn't we think that in the future it will adjust to the culture of its time? The dialogue between culture and religion is essential, as it was proposed by Vatican II. From the beginning, the Church has asked for a continuous conversion— *Ecclesia semper reformanda*—and that transformation takes on diverse shapes throughout time, without altering dogma. In the future there will be different ways of adjusting to new periods, just as today there are different ways from the times of regalism, of jurisdictionalism, of absolutism. You, Rabbi, also made an allusion to parochialization. That is a key, the trend toward a small community as a place of religious belonging. It responds to a need for identity, not only a religious identity, but also a cultural identity: I am from this neighborhood, from this club, from this family, I am from this religion . . . so I have a place of belonging, I recognize myself in an identity. The origin of Christianity was "parochial." When one reads Saint Luke's Acts of the Apostles, one notes that Christianity had a massive expansion; during Peter's first sermons they baptized two thousand people, who they later organized into small communities. The problem is when the parish does not have any life of its own and is absorbed into a higher level of the structure. What gives life to the parish is this sense of belonging. I remember, Rabbi, one day when I went to chat with you at your community and you took me to meet the women that do the social work at the synagogue. They were preparing packets and bags for needy families. The synagogue or the parish leads us to care for our brothers, these places move religion to action. In this case it was more of an act of welfare, but there are also other forms: educational, promotional, etc. For actions of this type, they accuse us of getting involved in things that, supposedly, should not interest us. A short time ago, for example, I celebrated a Mass in the Constitución station for the victims of human trafficking: slavery in sweatshops, exploited trash pickers, children used as drug pushers, and girls caught in prostitution. It ended up being a large protest, where non-Catholics gathered, who did not share my faith, but who shared the love for their brother. I am not entering into politics, I am entering the flesh of my brother, who was placed on the mincing machine, in a slave factory. It is true that some also take advantage of this to introduce politics; that is why it is important to discern how to act in those circumstances.

SKORKA: As Isaiah said, Do not "[turn] your back on your own flesh."[106]

BERGOGLIO: The translation that I use is "Do not be ashamed of the flesh of your brother." The religious relationship involves a commitment, not an escape. There was a period in Catholic Spirituality that existed that was called *fuga mundi*[107]; now the concept is completely different–it is necessary to engage the world, but always from the religious experience. You recently mentioned that when a phenomenon occurs in one religion, it also tends to happen in another. The problem is serious when the spiritual is reduced to the ideological, and the religious experience loses strength and leaves an emptiness, turning to the world of ideas to fill itself. The other risk is to do charity work for its own benefit, acting as an NGO instead of acting from

---

106 Isaiah 58:7
107 Ed. Note: Latin for "escape from the world" or search for a completely isolated, mystical life.

the religious experience. There are religious communities that run the risk of sliding unconsciously into an NGO. It is not only a question of doing such and such a thing to assist a neighbor. How will you pray? How will you help your community enter into the experience of God? Those are essential questions.

SKORKA: Looking back in retrospect, parochialism began to appear in the Jewish community about forty years ago. Until the end of the 1960s, there was a network of schools that passed on Jewish culture, and there were Zionist youth movements that imparted all kinds of lessons in Hebrew, history and tradition—but there were no major new developments in spirituality. It was at that time that the Conservative Movement in Argentina began to spread and the idea began to grow that the temple could be a place for children's activities as well as prayer. It is also where we could organize large campaigns to help neighbors in need. Another thing that I believe it is important for me to add is that in order to achieve a deeper religious experience in the future, our religious leaders will need to show much more humility. All people, when they teach their children, should clarify that they are talking about their own truth, their own religious beliefs, and that they would like for their descendants to enhance and perfect it. It is also absolutely improper to devalue and dismiss another person's religion and believe that only one's own represents the truth. If we can develop a truly humble attitude, we can change the world. When the prophet Micah wanted to define what it meant to be a religious man, he said to "do justice and to love goodness, and to walk humbly with your G-d."[108]

BERGOGLIO: I completely agree with the notion of humility. I also like to use the word *meekness*, which does not mean weakness. A religious leader can be very strong, very firm, but without exercising aggression. Jesus says that the one who rules must be like a servant. For me, that idea is valid for the religious person in any denomination. The true power of religious leadership comes from service. When the religious person stops serving, he begins to transform into a mere manager, into an NGO agent. The religious leader shares with, suffers with, and serves his brothers.

SKORKA: Exactly. I do not know what religion will look like in the future, but I am convinced that it depends on what we do today as individuals. Walter Benjamin once said, "I do not know if the book I am writing will have an impact today, but perhaps it will have an impact sometime in the next hundred years."

BERGOGLIO: I know that for religions there were worse periods than the current one, and nevertheless, they resurfaced. Perhaps now we can point to a numeric shortage of religious, but there were times when there was a shortage of virtue. There were corrupt times in the Church. I think, for example, about the times when the birthright existed, in the scholastic

108 Micah 6:8

benefits that some priests had, that secured their lives around instructing children from rich families. They did not do anything and they had become worldly. There were very difficult times, but religion bounced back. All of a sudden figures like Mother Teresa of Calcutta appeared, and they stirred up the concept of the dignity of the human person, figures who wasted their time–because in some way the time was lost–in helping people die. These actions generate mystique and rejuvenate religious fervor. In the history of the Catholic Church the true reformers are the saints. They are the true reformers, those that change, transform, carry forward and resurrect the spiritual path. In another case, Francis of Assisi contributed an entire concept about poverty to Christianity in the face of the wealth, pride and vanity of the civil and ecclesial powers of the time. He carried out a mysticism of poverty, of dispossession and he has changed history. In Judaism, how do these men appear?

SKORKA: One example I would mention is someone who was criticized widely throughout the Argentinean Jewish community for many things, but who undoubtedly marked a before and an after–Marshall Meyer. I cannot say that he was a saint because the concept of sainthood does not exist in Judaism; neither will I say that everything he did was perfect, nor do I agree absolutely with all of his points of view. But, if we take into account that the community began to flourish in the 1960s, it was thanks to him. Religion played a very important role in Marshall's character. No one can deny that there was a "before Marshall" and an "after Marshall," not only because of what he represented in the struggle for human rights, but because he showed us a new way of dealing with our neighbors, and for his having shaken the spiritual foundation of the Argentinean Jewish community. After he passed away and, more recently, say over the last twenty years, there has been another change. There has been a return to more orthodox forms of the religion. Thirty or forty years ago the present scenario would have been unimaginable–a return to a more strict way of practicing that contains many aspects with which I do not agree. Zygmunt Bauman, the well-known European sociologist who coined the phrase "liquid modernity," describes precisely the times in which we are living. He spoke about the lack of certainty and commitment in the world. Orthodoxy fills the gaps that are created by these uncertainties. The truth is that things keep going from one extreme to another. Regarding the future of religion, I believe it is vital that we find the middle path. Certain truths are firmly established like "do not kill" and "do not steal." On the other hand, change and freedom are part of life and one has to be able to think for oneself and distinguish right from wrong because the paths our lives will take are not set in stone.

BERGOGLIO: There are sectors within every religion that by highlighting the normative leave aside the human, they reduce religion to what has to be prayed in the morning, during the afternoon and at night and what is going to happen if one does not do it. There is a spiritual harassment of adherents and of many people weak in spirit, that can lead them to a lack of freedom. Another feature of these sectors is that they always are motivated by the search for power. Regarding Buenos Aires specifically, we can say that it is a pagan city, not in the derogatory sense, but as a matter of fact. It has many gods that it adores and, as a result of this paganization, it tends toward a phenomenon like the one that you mentioned. The authentic wants to be sought, but when that means only the normative, fulfilling regulations, it falls into the other extreme, into a purism that also is not religious. It is true that the hedonistic, consumerist, and narcissistic cultures have infiltrated Catholicism. They infect us and in some way relativize the religious life, paganize it, and make it worldly. That is what causes the watering down of religion; it is what I most fear. I always maintain that Christianity is a small flock, like Jesus says in the Gospel. When the Christian community wants to make itself great and transform itself into a temporal power, it runs the risk of losing the religious essence. That is exactly what I fear. Perhaps today someone can say that there are fewer religious people, but there is a lot of restlessness, there is a serious religious search. There is also a search for God in popular movements of piety that are forms of living the religious experience in a popular manner. For example, the pilgrimage of the youth to

Luján.[109] For many, the only time that they step into a church is when they make that procession: 60 percent go by themselves on that pilgrimage, they are not taken there by anyone from the parish. There is a spark of popular piety that summons them; it is a religious phenomenon that cannot be neglected. Maybe there are fewer people in the churches, but there is a purification of commitment. The religious search has not faded, it continues on strong, though somewhat disoriented outside the institutional structures. In my opinion, the biggest challenge that religious leaders have is in knowing how to guide that force. Evangelization is essential, but not proselytism; that today–thanks be to God–is crossed out of the pastoral dictionary. Pope Benedict XVI has a very beautiful expression: "The Church is a proposal that is reached by attraction, not by proselytism." It is about an attraction through testimony.

SKORKA: Judaism has never proselytized, but today there is a trend that I would call internal proselytizing. It is not about getting someone who is not Jewish to convert to a religious Jewish lifestyle, but instead

109 Ed. Note: Luján, Our Lady of Luján, located in the small town of Lujan, is approximately thirty miles west of Buenos Aires and is the most popular Marian Devotion in Argentina. The Archdiocese of Buenos Aires started a youth pilgrimage to this popular religious site in 1974. Each year, since then, more than 700,000 young people walk to the shrine in the month of October.

it is the Orthodox Jewish communities who are trying to bring their institutions to other Jews. But I want stop and go back to one of the things that you mentioned, Monsignor. Religious leaders ought to know how to handle each of those expressions of interest and how to guide those religious movements that appear spontaneously. It seems to me that that will be the function of religion in the future. I do not believe that a religious leader should have such a tight grip on his congregations, controlling them with an iron fist. That is only something G-d can do, who with a strong hand and an outstretched arm took the Children of Israel out of Egypt. Let us go back to the example of Marshall Meyer. When he was still with us, he was a very charismatic leader, but perhaps the Conservative Movement is now suffering due to the deep impact made by the centralization of our leadership. Maybe, due to the circumstances that marked his life, he had no alternative but to carry the weight of all that he had built on his shoulders and push forward on his own. However, that also prevented his followers from developing their full potential. Today, Argentinean life is different. It requires more subtle leadership and I do not like those leaders who are overly charismatic. To me, a religious leader is a teacher who should become incensed whenever a serious and unequivocal response is required to confront injustice. If we are to speak of having religious feelings as being an intimate experience, a teacher should not just make broad pronouncements but should have clear and concise words for each individual. I do not like egotism and selfishness, either in political leaders or religious ones. The use of mass instruction was an explicit part of recent religious movements that ended in huge massacres. That is why I think we have to be very careful when we are talking about new religious movements. When someone is bringing a new spiritual message, we have to treat it with the utmost respect, but at the same time it also merits the attention of responsible organizations who should study what it is all about. No movement's spiritual requirements should lead to conflict with one's family and it should not trap individuals inside any kind of web that is going to isolate them from their social or emotional network.

BERGOGLIO: I am respectful of all new spiritual proposals, but they must be authentic and submit themselves to the passage of time, which will reveal if their message is temporary or will live on through the generations. Surviving the passage of time is the major test of spiritual purity.